Hell Yeah Self-Care!

by the same authors

How to Understand Your Gender
A Practical Guide for Exploring Who You Are
Alex Iantaffi and Meg-John Barker
Foreword by S. Bear Bergman
ISBN 978 1 78592 746 1
eISBN 978 1 78450 517 2

Life Isn't Binary
On Being Both, Beyond, and In-Between
Meg-John Barker and Alex Iantaffi
Foreword by CN Lester
ISBN 978 1 78592 479 8
eISBN 978 1 78450 864 7

Gender Trauma
Healing Cultural, Social, and
Historical Gendered Trauma
Alex Iantaffi
Foreword by Meg-John Barker
ISBN 978 1 78775 106 4
eISBN 978 1 78775 107 1

Hell Yeah Self-Care!

A Trauma-Informed Workbook

Alex Iantaffi and Meg-John Barker

Jessica Kingsley Publishers
London and Philadelphia

First published in Great Britain in 2021 by Jessica Kingsley Publishers
An Hachette Company

4

Copyright © Alex Iantaffi and Meg-John Barker 2021
The figure on p.96 has been reproduced with kind permission from Geoffrey Roberts.

A CIP catalogue record for this title is available from the British Library and the Library of Congress

ISBN 978 1 78775 245 0
eISBN 978 1 78775 246 7

Printed and bound by CPI Group (UK) Ltd, Croydon CR0 4YY

Jessica Kingsley Publishers' policy is to use papers that are natural, renewable and recyclable
products and made from wood grown in sustainable forests. The logging and manufacturing
processes are expected to conform to the environmental regulations of the country of origin.

Jessica Kingsley Publishers
Carmelite House
50 Victoria Embankment
London EC4Y 0DZ

www.jkp.com

To Audre Lorde and all those who

continue to fight for liberation.

Until we're all free.

Acknowledgments

We are grateful first of all to the traditional custodians of the lands on which we have been raised, on which we currently live and where we have written this book. We are particularly grateful to all the Indigenous elders, activists and resisters who keep teaching us about interdependence and being in relationship to land and one another. We are thankful for all the community organizers, authors, activists, mentioned and unmentioned in this book, who have thought and written about this topic before us. Our work could not have happened without them.

We are also thankful to all those who have cared about us, throughout our lives, and for whom we have cared: individuals, groups, communities, ancestors, land, water, plants and animal companions.

Contents

.

Staying With Feelings

Somatic Self-Care

Selves Care (Your Plural Selves)

Self-Care and Other-Care

Reflections and Resources

Introduction

Why this book?

Why did we write this book? When we looked at the landscape of what workbooks were already out in the world, we felt that many of them targeted specific mental health difficulties, such as depression and anxiety. However, we noticed fewer—if any—resources available to help people to think more broadly about care for self and with others, and how to build it into their lives.

We believe that both receiving and giving care is essential to our mental health. At the same time, we take a critical perspective on traditional mental health approaches, which usually individualize problems through diagnosis. We much prefer the concepts of self-care and interdependent care highlighted by black, brown, Indigenous, feminist, disabled, and often trans and queer, scholars and activists. In those frameworks, self-care is a tool for survival, so that we can engage in the struggle for liberation again and again. We also acknowledge, throughout this book, that many of our struggles are systemic and rooted in structural inequalities, oppression, colonialism and repression of life and vitality.

No matter where we are or who we are, care can be pretty counter-cultural, especially when by care we mean interdependent care, in a world that pushes us to go faster, buy more and get ahead of "others." In our experience, we/people struggle with care for self and others, no matter what our mental health "labels" might be. So it seemed to make sense to combine our work in this area and bring you—the reader—a workbook about care.

Care, of self and others, can sustain us in times of crisis and trauma. However, it can only do so if it's already embedded in our lives and communities. Many people already know how to do this. Many people don't. If you lean towards the don't side, this book might be for you. If, as you're reading this, you find yourself feeling angry, that's good. There is a lot to be angry about in the world right now, and anger is mobilizing, it moves us towards actions. Too often, though, we've experienced people turning that anger in towards themselves. This could be because it wasn't safe to turn that anger outwards, at home, at school or in the wider world.

If you notice being angry about a book about self-care, take a moment to pause, breathe and ask yourself: Where is that anger coming from? Is it easier to direct that anger at us, or this book, because directing it at the world can feel so overwhelming? If that's the case, that's OK. After all, why are we talking about self-care in the apocalypse, right? Isn't self-care just selfish and privileged? Well, this is complicated. Taking care of self and others does require a certain amount of privilege, in terms of energy, support, access to finances and resources. This is true and we address this in the book again and again.

However, we do not think that truly caring for ourselves is inherently selfish. We're not talking about self-indulgence, and "oh go on, buy that gadget or those chocolates, you deserve it," in this book. If that is your self-care, that's fine. This is not what we're talking about here, it's not care as consumption. We've written this book because we believe we truly are all essential. And, if we are essential to the movement for liberation, we need to take care of ourselves and one another, as an integral part of the struggle, not as an afterthought. How can we fight the system when we're exhausted? How can we be effective in building community if we're so traumatized and reactive that we end up isolated or lashing out at our accomplices?

If we're marginalized, we need care to continue existing, knowing that our existence is resisting a dominant culture that wants us dead or so exhausted that they can easily push us aside. If we're privileged, can we be fully aware of what our agency is, and use that privilege to join the fight as full participants and as daring accomplices, as Indigenous activists have called on us to be? If we're a mixture of the two, as many of us are—privileged in some areas and marginalized in others—can we imagine a world of interdependent care, mutuality and kinship?

We wrote this book because we don't believe that suffering is in itself moral. If we're privileged, suffering will not purge or redeem us in some way from our unearned power in the world. This seems to us a colonial, Christian and puritanical way to view suffering. We do, however, believe in the vision that, as we stated earlier, many black, brown, Indigenous, feminist, disabled, and often trans and queer, scholars and activists have woven across time and space. This is a vision of liberation, of mutuality, of interdependence, of right relationships, of justice and of care. This is but a small offering to those ideals, to those visions, to those yearnings within us and in our communities.

Who are we?

So who are we to be writing a book like this? Always a good question to ask ourselves! We are both therapists, although one of us (Alex) sees clients and was trained in somatic, as well as talk therapy, and the other one (MJ) has moved towards offering writing mentorship services these days. It seems important to name this, given that part of our educational backgrounds, and our day-to-day work, is focused on care. We're also people who live with the legacy of developmental trauma and experience chronic and acute health conditions and disabilities. We're activists, community organizers and people interested in healing, justice and liberation movements. This means we think about care a lot, from many perspectives, for ourselves and with others. Care for self and others is part of our everyday lives, personally and professionally. Therefore, we hope that the range of academic, activist, therapeutic, personal and spiritual perspectives that we bring together do provide a lot of food for thought.

We want to be clear that we're not always brilliant at self-care. In fact, we struggle with it, in a range of ways. We don't always do all the things that are supportive of ourselves and others. There are many reasons—some individual and some systemic—why it's not always easy to care for ourselves and other people. We invite you to explore this for yourselves throughout the book. We want to share this point here because we don't want to give the impression that we've got this all figured out. We struggle with care, just like you probably do, if you've picked up or have been given this book. We share our struggles, and some solutions and approaches that we've found helpful for ourselves, our clients and communities, in our combined nine decades of life, across three different countries. We hope this offering is of use to you.

Who are you?

This is a great question, and you probably have a better answer for this one than we do! However, if we think about who our intended audience is, this is what we had in mind.

Our workbook is really for anyone interested in care. You might be a therapist, healer, community organizer, activist, teacher, a person living communally, an artist, someone struggling with mental health issues, or just someone who is interested in care, and who maybe doesn't know where to start, or who has tried everything out there already.

We hope that this workbook will be useful to you, wherever you are in the world. However, because of who we are and where we live, we also acknowledge that, despite our efforts, this workbook will, inevitably, mostly appeal and apply to "Western" audiences who speak English. Therefore, it might be most relevant to readers in the UK and US, as well as Australia, New Zealand, Canada and Western Europe. We understand that this workbook may be less applicable in countries beyond these, due to different cultural understandings of the self (although these will certainly be touched on, and challenged, through this workbook).

Generally, this book might be more appealing to you if you're interested in thinking about care from a more social, communal perspective, rather than just as an individualized pursuit of happiness and wellbeing. However, we truly think there may be something here for anyone, and that you might find the book useful whatever your idea of self-care might be right now. As we'll talk about in a moment, you might want to use this book alone or with others. You may be buying or borrowing this book for yourself, your clients, students or peers. Whoever you are, and wherever you are, we hope this book will be of service to your and your communities' wellbeing.

How to engage with this book

It's up to you how you want to work or play with this book. We've tried to structure it in a sensible way for those of you who'd like to go through it section by section, so that each section builds on the last. But it is also completely fine to dip into the book, even by picking a random chapter to focus on, or being guided by what speaks to you at the moment.

Generally, each page—or double page—introduces an idea with some kind of practice or activity, so it should be fine just to flick to a page and try something out. Also, some sections of the book may feel more or less relevant to you. It's fine to skip a chapter or section—for example, if you're not into body practices, then the section on somatic self-care may be less interesting to you, or if you don't resonate with the sense of plural and in-process selves, then the section on that may be one to skip over for you.

The only thing we would say is to go slow and gently with this workbook. Most chapters and pages introduce a lot of ideas and practices, so even one page could be enough for one day, or perhaps even a week if you want to let it sink in, and try something out a few times, or try a few different versions of the same thing. If you want to engage deeply, it could be great to give yourself a month to play with the ideas and practices in one section before moving on to the next.

Another thing you might like to do is to create an offline—or online—group to engage with the book. You could meet to try things out together, or to discuss how you found certain things. Something that we emphasize throughout the workbook is that self-care is difficult—if not impossible—without systems and structures of support. So sharing your thoughts and experiences in key relationships, and/or with a network of supportive people, can be a great part of cultivating those systems and structures of mutual care and supporting each other in self-care (see Chapters 21–24).

Before we introduce the structure of the workbook, let's just touch in on four points to keep returning to as you play with these ideas and practices. These are: different things work for different people at different times; open-handedness; addressing self-criticism around self-care; and the connection between self- and other-care.

Different things work for different people at different times

There are literally hundreds of different self-care practices mentioned in this workbook, and probably thousands more that you could find if you followed up all the resources at the end, or searched for other materials on self-care. This can be overwhelming, so why have we included so many?

The reason is that different things work for different people when it comes to self-care, and different things also work at different times of the same person's life. In fact, what may be self-caring for one person at one time may actually be the opposite of self-caring for another person, or at a different time for the same person.

Our dear friend H Howitt calls this the self-care/self-sabotage problem. Sometimes it can be really hard to tell the difference between the two. I'm shattered tonight, but will staying home and watching TV be just the rest that I need, or will it leave me feeling scratchy and annoyed with myself? I know that exercising can feel really good for me, but is making myself get up and go to a class when I'm not feeling it self-care or self-sabotage? Will spending time on social media rev me up or grind me down?

Instead of trying to find the "right" answer about which practices are "good" for you, and which are "bad," we encourage you to play with them, and also to learn how to feel into your body and emotions about what's best for you, at any given time (there's lots on how to do this in Chapters 9–16). For this reason, we've emphasized having *both* structure *and* flexibility throughout the workbook.

Even then, we won't always do what's best for us in any given moment. Sometimes we'll start something and realize that it isn't nourishing us. The material through the book on self-consent can help you to learn what that feels like to you, and how to become kinder to yourself around putting something down when it's not helping, and trying something else instead (see Chapters 4 and 23).

Open-handedness

What we've just said relates to an idea that we touch on several times throughout the workbook: open-handedness. What does it mean to hold anything—an idea, a practice, a relationship, a community—with open hands? We love this metaphor from Buddhist author Martine Batchelor:

> Let's imagine that I am holding an object made of gold. It is so precious and it is mine—I feel I must hold onto it. I grasp it, curling my fingers so as not to drop it, so that nobody can take it away from me. What happens after a while? Not only do my hand and arm get cramp but I cannot use my hand for anything else. When you grip something, you create tension and limit yourself.
>
> Dropping the golden object is not the solution. Non-attachment means learning to relax to uncurl the fingers and gently open the hand. When my

hand is wide open and there is no tension, the precious object can rest lightly on my palm. I can still value the object and take care of it; I can put it down and pick it up; I can use my hand for doing something else. (2001, p.96)

Applying this to self-care practices, we might try a new practice—a brief meditation practice, for example—and find that it leaves us in a wonderful, calm, contented state. We might then grasp that practice, deciding to get up early and do the practice for half an hour every day. After a week of finding that really hard, and being disappointed that we never reach that peaceful state again, we might hurl that practice away from us. We might even tell everyone that meditation sucks and come up with a bunch of reasons why it's not for us, and maybe why nobody else should do it either.

If we can hold that new practice with more open hands, instead of grasping and hurling it away, we can play with it and get curious about it. What was it about that first time that worked so well for us? What is it about the practice that appeals? Does it work better for us in certain contexts (like in a class or listening to a guided meditation, rather than alone)? Does it work better at certain times of day or for a certain length of time? We can try different versions of the practice. We can mix it up with other things (like reading, writing or talking with others). We can think about why we're doing it. We can remember that it's OK—in fact inevitable—that different things will work for us at different times. We can question what a practice "working" or "not working" for us even means.

Addressing self-criticism around self-care

The grasping and hurling-away manner of treating things is related to something else that we will talk about a lot through this workbook: self-criticism. We often grasp things because we're so critical of ourselves. We believe there's something wrong with us and we're searching for practices, relationships, communities, ideas and so on to fix us. Because we've grasped them so hard, this can often lead to us hurling them away when they disappoint us, or—often—when we feel as if we've failed at them in some way, and that is reinforcing the sense of ourselves as not good enough.

In a dominant culture that encourages us to be critical of ourselves all the time, it is really difficult for self-care not to become yet another thing to criticize ourselves for: we're not doing enough, we're not doing it right, we're not doing the best kinds of self-care, we're doing it too much, we shouldn't need it so much, we're self-indulgent for doing it, we don't deserve it, and so on, and so on.

We'll return to this several times during the workbook because it's such a common issue, but for now here are a few things to remind yourself of if and when you find yourself using self-care, or this workbook, as yet another stick to beat yourself with:

- Try to focus on forms of self-care that work well for you, that you find easy and pleasant enough to do.

- Explore where these messages that you're not OK or deserving come from, and get support with them.

- Share these struggles with trusted others who doubtless struggle too, and try not to use each other as a point of comparison, because they will struggle in similar and different ways to you.

- Gently laugh at the ridiculousness of being unkind with yourself about your struggles to be kind towards yourself!

The connection between self- and other-care

As we mentioned before, a major stumbling block with self-care is the common idea that caring for ourselves is selfish. However, we emphasize throughout this workbook that there is a major connection between self- and other-care, because we're all interconnected and interdependent.

Some people use the metaphor that self-care is a bit like applying our oxygen mask on an aeroplane before helping another person. We're not so helpful if we can't breathe ourselves! Here are just a few reasons why self-caring can mean we're in a better place to also care for others in our lives:

- We have more energy and capacity to offer if we're well rested and cared for.

- We see the situation more clearly if we take time for reflection, instead of going on autopilot and jumping to conclusions.

- We're more likely to know our limits and boundaries and not burn out.

- We won't get resentful because we're sacrificing ourselves too much.

- We're modelling that everyone needs and deserves care instead of acting as if some people—us—don't need or deserve it.

- We're treating ourselves as fellow human beings, instead of some kind of saviour or rescuer (which is patronizing, paternalistic and disempowering to the people we're trying to help).

- We'll be better able to handle criticisms or unforseen problems.

What's in this book?

So, what's in the rest of this book?

The first section, *Why Self-Care?* (Chapters 1–4), helps you to think more about whether self-care is a useful idea for you, and why it might be so important and challenging in the world today.

The next section, *What Is Self-Care?* (Chapters 5–8), introduces various different kinds of self-care practices which you might want to try. This includes basic self-care, kind and reflective self-care, and the routines and rituals we can use to build self-care into our lives.

Staying With Feelings (Chapters 9–12) focuses on emotions and gives you lots of ideas for exploring your relationship with your moods and feelings, and getting to know them better.

Somatic Self-Care (Chapters 13–16) is all about your relationship with your body, and somatic—or bodily—forms of self-care which you might want to do, including those relating to joy and pleasure. This section also touches on trauma, health and disability.

Selves Care (Your Plural Selves) (Chapters 17–20) introduces the ideas that we might be plural rather than singular, and in process rather than fixed, and provides a lot of possible practices for caring for the different sides of yourself, and for yourself past, present and future.

Self-Care and Other-Care (Chapters 21–24) returns to the idea that we're all interconnected and interdependent and explores how we can do relational self-care and cultivate systems and structures which support us in our self-care.

The final section, *Reflections and Resources*, provides a number of worksheets for you to use when planning your self-care from now on, as well as lots of further resources that you might want to engage with on this journey.

As mentioned, through the workbook we offer a diverse range of practices which you might build into your own self-care. For these, we are particularly drawing on the approaches we know well, which include: systemic, narrative and existential therapies; Buddhist mindfulness; Pagan ritual; trauma-informed and somatic practices; and intersectional feminism. We're aware that there are many other approaches to self-care, though, and we've tried to flag up other approaches which you might want to find out more about throughout, and in the further resources at the end.

We hope that you enjoy working, and playing, with this book as much as we've enjoyed creating it. Good luck on your self-care journey!

Why Self-Care?

CHAPTER 1

What Does the World Tell Us About Self-Care?

Take a moment to reflect on what self-care means to you. Where did you first hear these words? How do you feel about them? Write down a few words, if you like, or draw or get in touch with how it feels to think about self-care in this moment.

We believe that, in dominant Anglo cultures, these words have been used to turn care into a highly individualized enterprise. Feeling tired or suffering burnout? Maybe you're not doing enough self-care... You got sick? Maybe if you did enough self-care you wouldn't be sick... Have you ever received such messages or said those things? If so, what are they? Take a moment to fill the bubbles below with messages about self-care in the dominant culture you live in.

Take a moment to consider the messages you wrote down. Self-care might have become another buzzword to make us feel as if we're never enough or can never do enough of the "right things," such as meditation, bubble baths, yoga or whatever people around us tell us self-care is. In this context, self-care might feel obligatory and we might even feel judged by others for not doing enough "self-care." We might also be under the impression that if we did enough self-care, we would never get sick, be lonely or feel burnout, and that we would be happy and fulfilled.

Self-care can seem like the magic goal that everyone is looking for but few, if any, have achieved. Take another moment to list or draw below all the activities you can think of that might fall under the umbrella of "self-care" for you in this moment. Try to not overthink it, if you can!

This book is not self-care as another way to make you feel guilty about not being or doing enough.

This book is not about self-care as an individual responsibility.

This book will not tell you how to take care of yourself so that you're never sick again.

In this book, we reject non-consensual self-care as a means to the end of increased productivity and in service to capitalism.

No!

Using this book will not necessarily lead to greater happiness. In fact, we have no idea how this book might or might not affect you.

In this book, we strive to avoid reproducing ongoing settler-colonial violence. The land, green and red bloods (plant and animal life), including humans, are not things but rather living, breathing beings that deserve care and respect just because we exist.

We're not going to tell you what works for you but we hope to support you in discovering this for yourselves.

In this book, we're really talking about interdependence and care as mutual (both self and community, and is there even a difference? Spoiler alert: we talk about that later!)

Why did we start by putting a big NO on the third page of this chapter? Isn't that a bit negative, especially for a book about self-care? To be honest with you, reader, we had some conflicting feelings about writing a workbook about self-care. We believe that in the places where we live (the UK and Turtle Island on Dakota and Anishinaabe territories, currently known as Minnesota, US), self-care is used as a way to police and control us.

As we wrote earlier, self-care can be viewed as a way to make us happier, more productive and, if we're unhappy, well...we must be doing something wrong! So here's something you can buy to make it better. As you will read in the next chapter, we want to discuss self-care as a much more political statement, especially for those of us with marginalized identities and experiences. So, we did agree to write this workbook and we do hope you'll find it useful, but it might be a bit different from what you expected (or maybe it's exactly what you expected). For now, take a moment to breathe and reflect on why this book found its way to you in this moment.

Why self-care for you and why right now?

Take a moment to think about what you may be looking for... Or maybe someone else gave you this book. If so, what motivated them to give you this gift and what would you like to do with it now that you've read this far? Breathe into all of it. What do you notice? What are the thoughts, memories, sensations and feelings that emerge?

If you decide to keep using this book, we'd like to invite you to formulate an intention for your work with it. An intention is just a sentence, usually not too long so that you can remember it easily. It's often good to have an action verb, something you want to do, as part of your intention. For example, "My intention in using this book is to better understand what caring for myself and others means in this stage of my life." Now it's your turn. Write down your intention on the next page.

*My intention in using
this book is...*

. . . .

Now take a moment to say this with us...

This book is not a stick or a weapon!

Why are we asking you to say this? Because too many times we have experienced, for ourselves, how easy it is to beat ourselves up with the idea that we're not doing enough self-care, or that we're not doing it well enough, or that we're not doing the right kind of self-care. Once a therapist told one of us when taking a course: "This is not a self-improvement project, it's a self-acceptance one." We'd love for you to approach this book as a gentle invitation to dance with the idea of self-care, hold it with open hands and let go of anything that makes you feel as if you're not doing enough, or that you're not enough in any way. So, let's repeat one more time...

This book is not a stick or a weapon!

Whenever you feel you're being unkind to yourself, please don't use it as yet another way to make yourself feel bad; just breathe if you can. We can be so good at giving ourselves a hard time. Let's just notice this struggle together, come back to breathing and remind ourselves that we're enough. If you're not there yet (and believe me, most of the time, neither are we), let us tell you that you're enough. It's OK if you don't believe it yet. Let's act as if we're enough, just as we are. That is some powerful magic for ourselves and the world right there.

You are enough.

and yes, there's really nothing more to it than that...

CHAPTER 2

Audre Lorde and Self-Care as a Political Act

It's easy to think that self-care is the *last* thing that we need. The situation around us can feel so *urgent* that we imagine it would be better to put all of our time, energy and resources into helping others around us, fighting injustice or saving the planet. Or we may become so *overwhelmed* by all of the circumstances calling for our attention that we just give up and do nothing because we have no capacity.

In such precarious times, it's often the case that the tensions, conflicts and suffering playing out on a global scale are echoed in our communities and our interpersonal relationships. It's easy to end up with a sense of hopelessness and frustration and overwhelming feelings when we see this. We can either rush in too fast trying to address everything all at once, or we can burn out and give up.

Self-care as we're exploring it in this book is about finding a middle way between these two extremes: ways in which we—as individuals, networks, communities and cultures—can look after ourselves and others in the situations we find ourselves in.

This is an image we'll come back to several times over the course of this book. On the next page, you might want to write the challenging situations you're currently experiencing on each level, to remind yourself how easy it is to feel that sense of urgency or overwhelm.

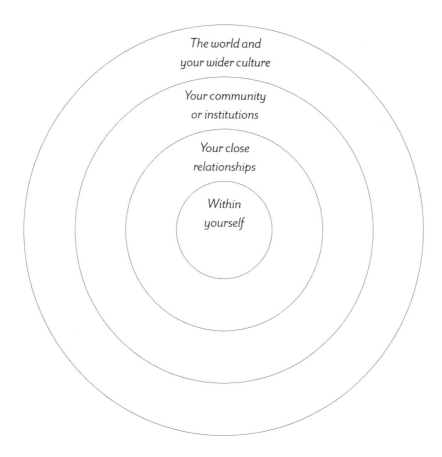

The world and your wider culture

Your community or institutions

Your close relationships

Within yourself

Things we might say to ourselves, facing this sense of urgency and overwhelming feelings, include:

"We need to do something now, not take time out for bubble baths!"

"Terrible things are happening to people, I need to focus on them, not me."

"My community is suffering and I just can't slow down right now."

"I'm finally realizing how much people like me—and the systems that privilege us—are part of the problem. I don't deserve self-care."

"Everyone looking out for number one is what got us into this mess."

Throughout this book, we'll return to the words of black feminist, Audre Lorde, on self-care. She said:

Caring for myself is not self-indulgence. It is an act of self-preservation and that is an act of political warfare. (2017, p.130)

Before we go on to unpack this idea a little further, think about it for yourself. How might caring for ourselves be an act of self-preservation? How might it be a political act?

Self-care as self-preservation

. . . .

. . . .

. . . .

. . . .

. . . .

. . . .

Self-care as a political act

. . . .

. . . .

. . . .

. . . .

. . . .

. . . .

Most of us are marginalized or oppressed in some areas, and privileged—or served by the systems around us—in others. Audre Lorde's quote is pointing to the fact that self-care can do two things. It can help us to:

- survive when we are marginalized or oppressed

- see injustice and do something about it when we are privileged or served by unjust systems.

Here are some of the ways self-care is important when we're marginalized or oppressed:

"Looking after myself means that I survive—
even thrive—in a world which doesn't seem to want
people like me to survive at the moment."

"Caring for myself demonstrates that people
like me are valuable even though we're
being treated as if we are disposable."

"Self-care gives me the energy to resist."

"When I look after myself, I have more energy to
look after others in my community."

"Pausing for self-care means that I pick my battles
more carefully so I have the time and resources to engage
in ways that are more likely to make a difference."

Make a note of some of the ways in which you—and the people around you—are marginalized and/or oppressed in your current culture. You might like to think about areas such as gender, race, class, sexuality, disability, age, geographical location, nationality, religion and indigeneity, and anything else that is relevant to your context. You can always keep adding to this.

Reflect on whether any of the quotes above make sense to you in relation to this, as reasons why self-care is important here. Is there anything else you would add?

. . . .

. . . .

. . . .

. . . .

Privilege means that the social structures and systems around us serve people like us better than other people. For example, if we're well-off, then we can afford to spend money to help us out of a situation when a crisis hits. If we're white, we don't have to fear violent responses from others, including those in authority, based on assumptions about the color of our skin. If we're straight, then we never have to "come out" about our sexuality because it's the one that is generally assumed. Here are some of the ways self-care is important when we're on the more privileged side of dynamics within our dominant culture:

"Looking after myself means I can see the ways I contribute to problems without crumbling under the weight of that knowledge. Then it's much easier to start doing things differently."

"When I care for myself, I notice I'm much more able to hear when people point things out about my behavior instead of getting defensive."

"Self-care means that I have the time and energy to protest, not just when issues impact me directly."

"Caring for myself gives me more empathy with people who are struggling with this stuff, just like I am."

"Self-care means that I can face the ways in which people like me have been oppressive towards other groups instead of trying to eradicate my 'inner oppressor' with violence towards myself."

Make a note of some of the ways in which you—and the people around you—are privileged in your current culture. You might like to think about areas such as gender, race, class, sexuality, disability, age, geographical location, nationality, religion and indigeneity, and anything else that is relevant to your context. You can always keep adding to this.

Reflect on whether any of the quotes above make sense to you in relation to this, as reasons why self-care is important here. Is there anything else you would add?

. . . .

. . . .

. . . .

. . . .

When things are so hard, it's easy to turn our exhaustion and frustration in on ourselves, especially within a wider culture that constantly tells us that we're unworthy, lacking and individually responsible for systemic issues. We'll say more about self-care as an act of resistance to this in the next chapter.

Lately, we've heard some people say that it would be a good thing if humans were eradicated by the forms of social collapse and/or climate crisis that we're currently facing, because we're an inherently "violent" and "parasitic" species. This can be another form of violence against ourselves. Instead of directly harming ourselves as individuals, we wish punishment on humanity more broadly, including ourselves. Yet this does not hold much larger systems, such as corporations or governments, responsible for their choices.

Part of self-care being a political act is remembering that humans are also an essential part of the ecosystem. Care is at the heart of healing justice frameworks which seek to find ways towards individual and collective liberation outside the current systems and structures that perpetuate oppression and violence.

One author who writes brilliantly about self-care, Naomi Ortiz, says in her book *Sustaining Spirit: Self-Care for Social Justice* (2018, p.14):

> Part of self-care is really about deepening our relationship with our own value. Activists can place their entire worth on what they are doing, what change they want to see in the world. This focus holds activists in an emotional stasis between working for change and holding hope for that change to occur. This stillness is where we must attend to ourselves.

Take a moment to breathe into the possibility that you have value just by existing, that you're deserving of care just because you are. Really let yourself breathe into that. Is it easy, uneasy or neutral? Is there comfort or discomfort in this idea? Breathe and notice. Then take a moment to write down any emerging thoughts, feelings, sensations and impulses when considering your inherent value.

CHAPTER 3

Criticism Culture and Self-Care

One of the main ways in which self-care is a political act is that it goes against the grain of how dominant society tells us to treat ourselves. We're calling this criticism culture.

Criticism culture encourages us to scrutinize and police ourselves at all times: to self-improve, to work on ourselves and to present a positive and successful self to the world.

This is linked to consumer capitalism, which is all about seeing ourselves as lacking and needing something to fill that lack. Advertising and many other forms of media create fears (e.g. we might look bad, be out of date or be a failure) and then offer products to allay those fears (e.g. beauty products, the latest fashion, recipes for success).

In such a culture, it's easy to end up constantly comparing our insides to other people's outsides. We often present curated versions of ourselves on social media: only the "good," "happy," "successful" images and stories and none of the "bad," "sad," "failure" ones.

Use the following page to write, draw or paste in the kinds of words and images that you see on a daily basis which encourage you to monitor yourself, compare yourself against others, see yourself as flawed and work on making yourself better. You might think about the images and messages in advertisements, online and offline magazines, reality TV shows, news, movies, pop songs and social media, for example.

Individualization is a big part of the picture when it comes to criticism culture. This means blaming ourselves—and other individuals—for problems that are actually structural or systemic. For those of us living under ongoing settler-colonial project structures, this is one way in which colonizing has seeped into our bodies, feelings and thoughts.

We know that social experiences such as poverty, discrimination, abuse and homelessness all take a great toll on mental health. Research consistently finds that marginalized and oppressed groups have worse physical and mental health than those in positions of privilege. However, criticism culture tells us that our struggles are our own individual fault, and it's our responsibility, as individuals, to fix them (e.g. by doing more self-care!).

We're encouraged to individualize things that are actually social problems, including our own suffering. This exacerbates our distress and means that we may well look in all the wrong directions when we try to address it: inwards instead of outwards.

Think about something that you struggle with—for example, you might pick something like worrying, drinking more than you want to, feeling bad about your body shape, losing your temper or working too hard. Write this in the box below and then try to come up with as many social and cultural reasons for this struggle as you can. No individual ones!

For example, for "feeling bad about your body shape," you might put things like: the dieting industry; fatphobic culture; restrictive white, Western beauty standards; my family's attitude towards food; school bullying.

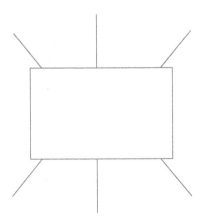

In such a culture, we often develop strong inner critics which tell us things like:

- We're flawed, lacking, bad or wrong.

- We need to monitor ourselves the whole time and compare ourselves to others.

- We must present a good front—or mask—to the world rather than our real self.

- Everything that happens to us is our own individual fault.

- It's our responsibility to make ourselves better.

You might like to draw an image of your inner critic here, and the kinds of things it says to you.

The inner critic can become so harsh and loud that we are extremely hard on ourselves (and often others), working more and more to better ourselves. Or we can give up entirely because it's such an impossible task. Take a breath and reflect on which of these feels most familiar to you. Or perhaps you swing between the extremes of being hard on yourself and giving up, as many of us do?

Self-care can be an important counter-balance to criticism culture and the inner critic for the following reasons, and more:

- It can teach us how to be kind instead of critical.

- We can learn to notice more easily toxic messages and injustices and their impact.

- It can enable us to be more vulnerable and less defensive.

- We can feel more connected with others and less isolated.

- We can become less focused on self-monitoring and therefore more able to turn outwards towards the world.

- If we spend less time and resources on "self-improvement" or perfecting ourselves, we may have more to offer.

- We can have less toxic shame and fear of others triggering this.

Our inner critic can come and/or be nourished from a range of places. We have already touched on popular culture (what we hear in songs, watch on TV and at the movies, read in comic books and so on), but we can also think about our communities and family of origin here. All these systems have their own norms and expectations around self-care: whether it's valid, if you should do it or not, and what counts as self-care.

These norms and expectations can be passed on horizontally—for example from peer to peer or sibling to sibling—or vertically—from parent to child or elders to youth. When these norms and expectations are held lightly and with open hands, our experiences can be expansive and even deviate from these norms and expectations. However, when these norms and expectations are rigid, we might feel constrained.

As well as norms and expectations around self-care, we can also experience the effects of intergenerational and systemic trauma in our lives. Sometimes this means that we might feel as if there is "something wrong with me," whereas what we're experiencing is not individual but systemic and/or intergenerational. For example, it's not "a personal failure" if we don't thrive as a person of color in a racist, capitalist society. Our "failure" is the product of larger systems of oppression. If we struggle as a first-generation college graduate and we notice others breeze ahead of us, it might be due to lack of intergenerational social capital, and so on. There are so many examples of how our capacity to care for ourselves and others might be impacted by forces much larger than us!

Take a moment to reflect on how systemic and intergenerational stories of oppression, healing and resistance might open up or close down opportunities for you to care about yourself in this moment. Some stories might open up some things, while closing down others. Remember, nothing is ever as polarized or binary as we might think! For example, if I come from a working-class family, this might close down my capacity to access vacations and rest, as I might view those as quite privileged things.

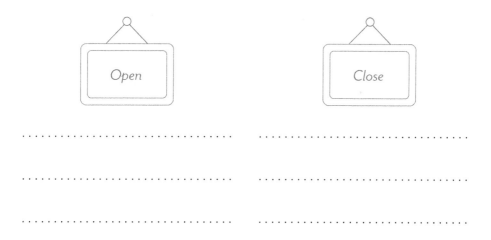

Why are we even talking about intergenerational and systemic trauma patterns in a book about self-care? We believe that our capacity to care for ourselves and others can be deeply impacted by intergenerational and systemic trauma. We also believe we can benefit from intergenerational wisdom, healing and care, if we are able to access it. If we're not careful, we risk re-creating, in our everyday lives, the same patterns of violence and oppression that we are trying to change through our work and/or activism:

- We might feel a sense of urgency, spurring us on to go *fast*. By doing so, we might not notice who gets left behind or doesn't even get to join us at the table.

- We might find ourselves being quite *harsh* and *judgmental* towards ourselves and others.

- We might also feel as if we're never doing *enough*, which then feeds both urgency and self-judgment.

- Finally, we might find it hard to be *consensual* with ourselves and others, if we're going so fast and pushing so hard to "get somewhere," wherever this might be.

Self-care can help us slow down and notice when we want to accelerate, when we're not paying attention to ourselves or others, when we're perpetuating patterns of oppression and abuse in our everyday lives and relationships, while being dedicated to and passionate about eradicating them. As Naomi Ortiz (2018, p.14) reminds us in the quote in Chapter 2, the "stillness" between "working for change and holding hope for that change to occur" is "where we must attend to ourselves," because it's in this stillness that we can make slower, more considerate choices about how we want to live our lives.

What would happen if taking care of ourselves could have unforeseen consequences for generations yet to come? What kind of ancestors are we going to be when it comes to self-care? What inheritance do we want to leave, not just to our biological descendants, which we may or may not have, but to our descendants of spirit, art, activism, to the trees, plants, bodies of water and rocks that will still be here after our choices are long gone?

Take a moment to imagine yourself as an ancestor. What kind of ancestor do you imagine yourself to be? What is your legacy not just to people but to the land, plants, water and rocks around you? What choices have contributed to this legacy? Take a moment to write down, draw and/or notice what comes up for you when you ask yourself these questions.[1]

---

1   We want to acknowledge the influence and presence of Colleen Cook, now an ancestor of activism, for this activity.

CHAPTER 4

The Cradle of Kindness

In the last chapter, we bullet-pointed four ways in which we often reproduce criticism culture if we're not careful. Let's remind ourselves of those points:

- Going too *fast* for ourselves and/or others due to a sense of urgency.

- Being *harsh* and *judgmental* towards ourselves and/or others.

- Feeling that we and/or others are never doing *enough*.

- Being *non-consensual* with ourselves and/or others.

If we want to build rhythms and rituals, systems and structures of self-care into our lives, we need to do this in a cradle of kindness. Such a cradle is a radical counter-balance to criticism culture.

Over the next few pages, we'll consider four elements of this cradle which counter each of the four points above. You might see these as the four legs supporting the cradle of kindness.

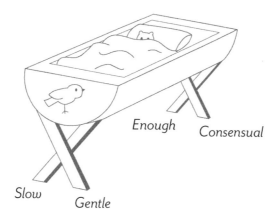

Enough   Consensual

Slow   Gentle

The first leg of the cradle is *slow*. However, given that many of us reading this book live under capitalism and dominant cultures that encourage us to go faster and do more, how can we slow down, even if for a moment? Even if we know how to slow down, we might find it hard to do so. We might see it as a waste of time or we might feel overwhelmed by our own emotions. Sometimes going fast can also be about running away from ourselves, so slowing down can be scary! We'll talk more about this when we discuss emotions, but, for now, let's focus on the slowing-down part, even if just for a few moments.

Choose an activity that you do on most days, almost without thinking. This could be showering, eating breakfast, drinking tea or coffee, petting your dog or cat, going to the bathroom and so on. Just make sure to pick an everyday activity that feels almost automatic to you. Got it? Write down what you picked, if you like.

. . . .

Next time you do this activity, slow down as much as you're able. For example, if you picked drinking tea, notice picking up your tea. Is the cup warm? How does it feel in your hands? Does the tea have a smell? What is it and is it a pleasant, unpleasant or neutral smell? Is there steam rising from the cup of tea? How does that impact you? Is it fogging your glasses? Does it feel comforting on your skin? Once you have thoroughly explored how the cup of tea feels in your hands, how the tea smells and how the steam rising from the tea feels, take the cup to your lips. How does the contact between the cup and your lips feel? Really notice what comes up for you even before the tea touches your lips. Once you start drinking the tea, how does the liquid feel against your lips and then in your mouth? You might want to slow down before swallowing the tea to really notice as many sensations as possible. Keep drinking your tea slowly, savoring and noticing each moment, as much as you're able.

How does it feel to slow down such an everyday activity? What thoughts, sensations and emotions rise in you? What does your body want to do? Is this comfortable, uncomfortable or neutral? Take a moment to write down your reactions to the slowing-down activity.

THE CRADLE OF KINDNESS

The second leg of the cradle is *gentle*, instead of harsh and judgmental. This too can be a challenging option to consider. We might view gentleness as being gendered, or weak, depending on the cultural messages received, and these may or may not fit with our self-image. Or we might consider gentle to mean nice and non-confrontational or conflict avoidant, which may also fit or not fit with our own sense of who we are.

By gentle, in this context, we mean compassionate and tender, vulnerable and open. We can be gentle and direct. We can engage in conflict and be gentle. When we're being gentle, we're more able to pick our battles because we're not coming from a place of reactivity. When we're gentle, we can also be more relational. We can be more curious and open; we're more able to ask questions and to listen to another person. There are, of course, situations in which gentleness is not possible. If we're under threat, we cannot be gentle. We can only be slow and gentle, or indeed any of the four legs of the cradle of kindness, if there's enough safety in our lives, as we'll discuss later in this book.

For now, let's go back to gentle. How can we cultivate gentleness in our lives? We invite you to consider starting with yourself. Notice the things you might say to yourself that are harsh and judgmental. Try to not beat yourself up for noticing just how harsh you can be with yourself. Just write it down. Then try to find a gentle way to respond to that harsh statement. For example, if one of the harsh phrases is "I'm lazy," you might respond with "Everybody gets tired now and then, it's OK to rest." Now give it a go with three or four of your own statements.

Harsh statement   **Gentle response**

. . . .

. . . .

. . . .

. . . .

Now take time to notice when you tend to be harsh with yourself and/or others. Are there reasons for this? For example, do you feel under threat or insecure, are you hungry or tired? Are there conditions that make it easier or harder for you to be gentle with yourself or others? What are the elements that nourish gentleness in your life?

The third leg of the cradle of kindness is knowing that we're *enough*. Once more, this can be a challenge if we're told we're never enough or never do enough. Depending on how we were brought up, this might indeed feel like mission impossible!

There is no shortcut here. We need to practice telling ourselves that we're enough. Every day, several times a day, again and again:

I am enough. I am enough. I am enough. I am enough.

I am enough. I am enough. I am enough. I am enough.

I am enough. I am enough. I am enough. I am enough.

I am enough. I am enough. I am enough. I am enough.

I am enough. I am enough. I am enough. I am enough.

I am enough. I am enough. I am enough. I am enough.

I am enough. I am enough. I am enough. I am enough.

I am enough. I am enough. I am enough. I am enough.

I am enough. I am enough. I am enough. I am enough.

I am enough. I am enough. I am enough. I am enough.

I am enough. I am enough. I am enough. I am enough.

And on those days when you can't tell yourself, maybe you can look at this page and breathe it in: **you are enough**.

The fourth leg of the cradle is about treating ourselves, and each other, *consensually*.

Consent is when we agree to do something. In order to be in consent, we need to be able to:

- tune in to how we feel—what we need and want, and where our limits and boundaries are

- communicate about this with others, knowing that we are free enough, safe enough and able to be honest, and that our position will be heard and respected.

We'll say a lot more about self-consent, and consent with others, in Chapter 23, but for now think about what conditions make you feel most able to tune in to your wants and needs, limits and boundaries, and communicate about them with others. You might reflect on a particular relationship—or situation—when you noticed that you found it easy to tune in to yourself and communicate with another person or people. We've given a couple of examples here so you can see the kind of thing we mean:

- When we had a monthly walking group, we made it easier for everyone to be in consent because we had an agreement that it was always fine for people to be there or not, we recognized our different access needs and checked in during the walk how people's bodies were feeling, and we said it was always fine for someone to come along but not chat if they weren't feeling up for that, or just to join us for part of the walk.

- When we write our books, we try to be consensual with ourselves and each other by pausing regularly to check in with our bodies and feelings, by reminding each other that consent is the aim, not getting so many words down on paper, and by giving ourselves different options for how we might work each particular day, recognizing that our energy levels and focus can vary.

Now take a moment to write your own example below, or make a mind map of relevant words or phrases:

If you've read some of our other books, such as *How to Understand Your Gender* (2017) and *Life Isn't Binary* (2019), you may already be familiar with the idea of slow down pages. This is a moment for you to slow down and not rush through this book, unless you want to, of course. Slow down pages are just invitations. In our previous books, we suggested activities, but this time we want to take a "Make Your Own" (M.Y.O.) approach so that you can slowly start to create a map of activities you enjoy.

What is one way in which you could slow down and take care of yourself right now? You may want to write it down or draw it to remember what you did. This space is for you. We'll see you again when you're ready.

M.Y.O. Slow Down Page

What Is Self-Care?

CHAPTER 5

Meeting Our Basic Needs and Why That Can Be Hard

In the last chapter, we mentioned the cradle of kindness and the elements that support it. However, it's hard to access our capacity to slow down, be gentle, feel that we're enough, and be consensual with ourselves and others if our basic needs are not met.

What are those basic needs, though? Let's start from our physiological needs, given that we're embodied. We all need to eat in a way that nourishes us, drink enough water to stay hydrated, and be able to sleep. In order for the latter to work, we also need access to a safe-enough shelter.

Those needs—eating nutritious food, drinking water, a safe-enough shelter and sleep—are non-negotiable pillars. If we don't meet those needs, we suffer. Yes, it's that simple. We can push through for a period of time but eventually we crumble if we're not meeting these basic needs. However, meeting those needs can be challenging at times for a number of reasons, from systemic poverty to the impact of trauma. We can't solve systemic poverty in a book but we'll talk about the impact of trauma later in this chapter.

For now, let's take a moment to assess where you're at with these basic needs. Please take a moment to fill in the table on the next page. We do understand that separating systemic from internal obstacles is a little bit of a forced duality, given that the two are connected, so if this doesn't work for you, feel free to reflect on it in a different way. Remember that you're always free to adapt any of the activities in this workbook to better suit your needs.

Needs	Systemic obstacles (e.g. not enough money for rent; noisy neighborhood; no supermarkets nearby)	Internal obstacles (e.g. it's hard to go to bed in a timely way; forgetting to eat; not enjoying drinking water)	On a scale of 1–10 how much are those needs met? 1 = not at all 10 = completely met	Are there changes towards meeting those needs that are under my control?
Food				
Water				
Shelter/ Housing				
Sleep				

We mentioned that trauma can get in the way of meeting our basic needs so we'll use the rest of the chapter to discuss trauma: how it might affect our basic needs and what we can do to address this (on a good day, as we acknowledge that trauma is much more complex than what we can discuss in a few pages!).

First of all, what is trauma? This word, originating from the Greek for "wound," started to be used in the late 17th century. Peter Levine, founder of Somatic Experiencing®, in his book *Healing Trauma: A Pioneering Program for Restoring the Wisdom of Your Body,* writes: "Although humans rarely die from trauma, if we do not resolve it, our lives can be severely diminished by its effects. Some people have even described this situation as a 'living death'" (2008, p.32). He also says, "What I do know is that we become traumatized when our ability to respond to a perceived threat is in some way overwhelmed. This inability to adequately respond can impact us in obvious ways, as well as ways that are subtle" (2008, p.3).

Another author, Jon Allen, writes in *Coping with Trauma: A Guide to Self-Understanding*:

> It is the subjective experience of the objective events that constitutes the trauma... The more you believe you are endangered, the more traumatized you will be... Psychologically, the bottom line of trauma is overwhelming emotion and a feeling of utter helplessness. There may or may not be bodily injury, but psychological trauma is coupled with physiological upheaval that plays a leading role in the long-range effects. (1999, p.14)

We want to make one thing very clear at this point. Trauma is not your fault and your trauma responses, which we'll discuss next, are not always under your control, especially once you're out of your window of tolerance, another concept that we'll discuss later in this chapter.

Pause a moment to take all of this in and reflect on whether any of this resonates for you. Trauma can be a really big word to use, so notice if you're having a reaction to this word. If so, what's the reaction you're noticing? Do you have a sense of where it comes from? Now take a moment to write down or draw or sense into your own definition of trauma.

Trauma is...

We've talked briefly about what is trauma and we have included some resources at the end of the book if you want to delve deeper into this. Right now, let's take a moment to think about recognizing our trauma responses as these might sometimes get in the way of meeting our basic needs. You might already know about the "classic" trauma responses of fight, flight and freeze. Some people, such as Pete Walker, author of *Complex PTSD: From Surviving to Thriving*, talk about the fourth F of trauma responses, "fawning," also known as people pleasing.

How do you recognize if you're in a trauma response? When in *fight*, we might feel hot and our heart might start racing. When in *freeze*, we might feel glued to the spot, unable to get away, When in *flight*, we might feel like running away. When in *fawn*, we might have the sensation of walking on eggshells or being highly vigilant. These are just examples and, in a moment, we'll ask you to think about how you personally experience those reactions. You don't need to have experienced trauma to access these experiences. They're part of our nervous system and survival mechanisms. You can also experience more than one reaction at once. For example, you might feel really revved up and wanting to escape or fight inside, but glued to the spot at the same time.

Now let's map these reactions in yourself. Take a moment to identify sensations, emotions, thoughts and impulses (i.e. what your body wants to do) for each of the four Fs: fight, flight, freeze and fawn. You can use the outline below to connect your reactions to different sensations in your body, or make a bigger outline of your own body, or just list what you notice for each reaction.

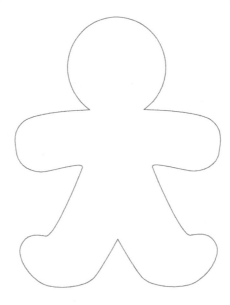

You might also notice that sometimes you dissociate. Some people might feel scared by dissociation. However, this, like the other trauma responses, is just another survival mechanism available to us. When we "zone out" while driving or walking to a familiar place, for example, or doing a familiar activity, that is a form of dissociation. Take a moment to notice how dissociation shows up for you. Is it a feeling of light-headedness, losing time, zoning out, not remembering all the details of an event? Notice and try to be as gentle and curious as you can during this process. You might add what you notice to the body map you've already worked with, if you like.

When we're not having a survival/trauma response (one of the four Fs, or dissociation), we're in what psychologists call our "window of tolerance." This is that space in our nervous system where we can be present and engaged with ourselves and the world around us. If we're having a survival/trauma response, it usually means that we're out of our window of tolerance. We might still be pretty close to the threshold of our window of tolerance, having just gone past it, or we might be really far away from that threshold. Sometimes we can go far out from our window of tolerance pretty fast, almost as if we're catapulted out of it suddenly, especially if we have a complex trauma history.

Boundaries are usually best and most easily set when we're within our window of tolerance. Of course, to be able to do this we need to know what our window of tolerance is, notice the signals when we're getting close to its edges and know what boundaries are helpful for us. This is not easy for many of us, as dominant culture doesn't always teach us best practices around consent, including self-consent and care for ourselves and one another, as we covered earlier. Let's try to notice what our window of tolerance feels like first. Please take a few moments to breathe into and notice how it feels to be present and engaged with yourself and others. Then write down or draw a few keywords/symbols around the image on the next page to remind you what your window of tolerance feels like for you.

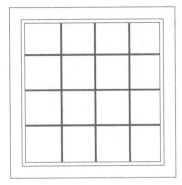

What are some of the things you can do when you're out of your window of tolerance? The main idea is to come back to some sense of safety. Depending on your history, identities and experiences, you may not feel 100 percent safe but you can come back to your own baseline, where things should feel somewhat manageable.

One of our favorite exercises to come back to the present is the following. Take a moment to notice five colors right in the space where you are and name them out loud (or in your head if you can't speak out loud right now), then do the same with four shapes, three textures, two things you can hear and one you can taste or smell. Please adapt this activity according to the senses available to you.

Another way to come back to yourself and the present is to gently (*gently* is important here) pat, squeeze or stroke your arms and legs for a few moments. This can help us come back to our very first boundary, our skin and body, the most organic boundary that just exists without us needing to do anything but be there.

Our body, our skeleton, muscle and skin are our very first boundary. If someone, including medical doctors, invades this without our consent, it can feel quite shocking. Taking care of our basic, physical needs then means taking care of our very first boundary. Honoring our most basic needs for food, water, shelter and sleep is to honor the boundary of our body. However, this can be challenging, especially if we're not doing well.

In times of crisis, it's important to have a special plan, such as a Wellness Recovery Action Plan®, also known as WRAP®, a self-designed wellness and prevention process. You might want to make a little zine or set of pages under the themes listed below. You can create them as mind maps, drawings or bullet-point lists, whatever works for you. It can be a great idea to share them with the people around you—and see theirs—so that you can help each other out if and when a crisis hits. They can be living documents which you add to over time as you learn more about yourself. The themes include:

MEETING OUR BASIC NEEDS AND WHY THAT CAN BE HARD

- *Everyday basics*: the daily basics that generally keep you in an OK place.

- *Extra good things*: things that often help you stay grounded and OK.

- *Triggers*: things you know can tip you into crisis or trauma response.

- *Warning signs*: things that often happen when you're starting to struggle, which you, and others, might notice.

- *Crisis management*: things you can put in place which often help once you've begun to get distressed. You can divide these into different sections for different levels of crisis, for example. You might also want to note down what doesn't help, or tends to make things worse.

When we're not in crisis, something that can support us in meeting our basic needs is having some routines around them. Routines help us save mental and emotional energy. Given that there is only so much decision power to go around every day, routines help us to reduce the amount of decision power we need to use to meet our basic needs. For example, if I have a routine around food preparation, that saves quite a lot of energy. If I keep a regular sleep schedule and bedtime routine, this can help reduce stress or even maintain my ability to meet my basic needs, even when I might be struggling emotionally. Routines mean that we don't need to reinvent the wheel of meeting our basic needs every day, which frees us up to spend that energy elsewhere.

Let's take some time right now to reflect on what routines you might have or wish to have around meeting the basic needs we introduced at the beginning of this chapter. Fill in the table below with ways in which you currently meet each of these needs and also any desired ways to meet those needs. There may or may not be any differences between these two.

Needs	Current	Desired
Food		
Water		
Shelter/Housing		
Sleep		

CHAPTER 6

Kind Self-Care

In Chapters 6 and 7, we're going to divide self-care into two types: kind self-care and reflective self-care. Once our basic needs are, ideally, met, these are the two types of self-care we might want to build into our daily lives. Kind self-care involves cultivating compassion towards ourselves, grounding ourselves in our everyday lives and just being. Reflective self-care is about taking time to reflect on how we do things, what our values are and how we want to live and relate with ourselves, others and the wider world.

As we mentioned in Chapter 4, we need the cradle of kindness before we start reflecting on these things. Otherwise, we easily rush, become harsh, judge ourselves for not being enough, and treat ourselves and others non-consensually. However, reflective self-care also feeds back into kind self-care, because it is in reflection that we may realize that we're not treating ourselves kindly, that we need more space or solitude in our lives, or that our harsh treatment of ourselves is also meaning that we treat others harshly, for example.

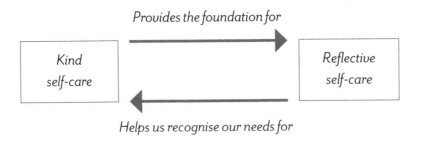

Before we give you lots of ideas, take a moment to consider what kind and reflective forms of self-care you might already have in your life. Kind self-care is anything you do that is gentle, soothing or grounding. Reflective is anything that gives you a chance to reflect on aspects of your life. Both can be things you do alone and/or with others. It doesn't matter if you can't think of anything yet, as there are lots of examples coming your way over the next few pages.

Kind   **Reflective**

. . . .

. . . .

. . . .

In criticism culture—with the strong inner critics that most of us have developed—it's very tempting and easy to do the opposite of kind self-care, especially when we're not feeling good about ourselves.

What things do you do that are self-cruel? How might you do something different? We've given you several examples in the table below which you can add to. Please remember, though, that different things count as self-cruel and self-kind for different people, and even on different days for the same person. It's much more about *how* it feels for you than it is about *what* you're doing.

For example, social media or watching TV are not inherently self-cruel or self-kind. For one person, social media may feel self-kind because they've curated a mutually supportive network, and checking in with their lives a couple of times a day leaves them feeling nourished (self-kind). For another, social media is something they do whenever they don't want to be with uncomfortable feelings, and they notice they often see something that makes them feel more worked up (self-cruel). One day, watching TV might be just the downtime you need; another day it might be more self-kind to spend some time with a friend or move your body.

Self-cruel	Self-kind
"I check my phone last thing at night when I'm tired already."	"I leave my phone in another room so I can't check it. It's easier to get to sleep."
"I stay in bed till the last moment so every day starts with stress."	"I spend 30 minutes in a cafe before work. It's easier to get up for a treat, and I start the day calmer."
"I go round and round things in my head thinking I could've done better."	"When this happens, I message a friend who gets it, and we support each other."
"I try to do all the activism in order to feel good about myself and then I burn out and can't do anything."	"I'm trying to focus on what I enjoy and what I'm skilled at instead of doing all the things."

Because our bodies and brains have often learned the self-cruel ways of doing things over a long time, it also takes time to shift them. Go easy on yourself. It's fine just to notice you've fallen into an old habit initially. Slow, gradual changes are more likely to stick.

Notice the pattern, do it differently, make that your journey.

What about developing specifically kind forms of self-care? In criticism culture, kindness can be a major act of resistance. It demonstrates to us that we're worthy of kindness no matter what, and it's also a good way to practice being kinder to others. Here are some ideas for self-kindness that you could build into your life. You might like to pick one to try today, and reflect later on how that was for you.

Daily kindness	Do one thing each day which is deliberately kind to yourself. Small things are great—for example, hot chocolate, your favourite sandwich for lunch, time with an animal, listening to your favourite music, cute animal videos online, re-reading a book you love, messaging a friend.
Daily remembering	Last thing at night, remember three things from the day that you're pleased with yourself for. Small things are great—for example, smiled at that person on the bus, did the washing up, made nice food.
Kind groups	Join or set up an online or offline group to share kind ideas, offer kindness to each other or get together to do kind things.
Kind planning	Look at the year ahead with kindness in mind. What things might you plan that are good for you—for example, kind people, places, events or activities? What less kind things might you let go of over time?
Objects, pictures, playlists	Take photographs, keep objects or make collages, Pinterest boards or playlists related to things that make you smile, good memories or kind things people have said to you.
Kind journal	Make your own journal or mini-zine of small things that lift your mood, such as items of clothing to wear, song lyrics, quotes, images.

If you picked one of these to try, reflect on how that was. Did you find it easy or hard to do? What blocks or obstacles did you experience, if any? What did you like about it? What didn't you like? How were you left afterwards? Feel free to adapt and add to the list for what works for you.

Remember to be kind about kind self-care! You don't have to do all the things on the list or even any of them; it's about what works for you and for your life. In criticism culture, it's so easy to use self-care as another stick to beat ourselves with. Go gently.

An important part of kind self-care is about giving ourselves moments for...
just being.

This is the idea that it's kind to spend some time in our lives "being" rather than "doing." It's sometimes called "mindfulness" or "being present," but those words can come with cultural baggage, and may also still give us an idea that there's a special set of techniques to it or something. Really, it's about anything that enables you to just be with who you are and what is happening right now in this moment.

Just being is a good way to get to know ourselves and our habits better, to slow down and notice things around us, to show respect for our feelings (rather than trying to get rid of them), and to counter the capitalist idea that we're only valuable and acceptable if we're producing something or doing something active. Here are some ways to practice being. The hot drink practice in Chapter 4 is another good one. We've tried to provide examples which work for all access needs, so please pick ones that work for your body and brain capacities. Most people find that focusing on certain senses works better for them.

Bird practice	Sit or stand somewhere you can see a fairly spacious outside area. Each time you see a bird, use that as an opportunity to come back to the present moment.
Audio meditation	Find one of the many free audio meditations that you can try online or through apps, and do that.
Bench	Spend ten minutes on a park bench, or sitting on the floor at home, just listening to the sounds around you. You can also watch the leaves on the trees or a candle flame if visual things work better than audio.
Stretching	Do some stretching for a few minutes. Focus on how your body feels.
Bath/shower	Have a bath or shower, paying attention to the feeling of the water on your body.
Breathing space	Any time you want, take three conscious breaths in and out. Notice the sensations in your body as you do so.
Plants	Take a short walk around your neighborhood noticing any plants. You might like to observe their colors, smells and textures.

If you picked one of these to try, reflect on how that was. Did you find it easy or hard to do? What blocks or obstacles did you experience, if any? What did you like about it? What didn't you like? How were you left afterwards? Feel free to adapt and add to the list for what works for you.

Here's an opportunity. Hold this page in your hand and...

Just Be

How was that?

. . . .

. . . .

. . . .

. . . .

. . . .

. . . .

. . . .

. . . .

. . . .

. . . .

⤙∾⤚

CHAPTER 7

Reflective Self-Care

As we said in Chapter 6, reflective self-care can be hard to do if we don't have the basics of self-care in place: being safe enough and having some kindness towards ourselves. If we don't have these things, it can be easy for reflective self-care to become a bit harsh.

If you find yourself being judgmental about fitting in reflective self-care, or find that reflecting on yourself becomes an exercise in self-monitoring and self-policing, then we'd recommend going back to some of the kinder practices or weaving them in with reflective self-care—for example, starting and ending your reflective time with a kindness or just-being moment. Here are some ideas for self-reflection that you could build into your life. You might like to pick one to try today, and reflect later on how that was for you.

Journaling	Write about your life and feelings. There are many different ways to do this, covered in Chapter 19 and the resources at the end of the book. You might try first writing a full description of what is happening and how it feels—however it comes out— then writing about how you're making sense of it and what you might do.
Peer-to-peer listening	Create a listening partnership with a friend where you each give the other time to say what's on your mind and talk about it. Nancy Kline's (1999) *Time To Think* is a good resource on how to do this.
Wandering and wondering	Moving the body can help thoughts and feelings to move through us. You might want to combine reflecting with a long walk, a swim or whatever other movement works for you. If talking aloud helps, you can always put on headphones as if you were on the phone!
Sharing circles	Create a group which meets regularly to share what's going on for members. You take it in turn to have five to ten minutes to say where you're at and everyone else just listens.
Thinking time	Make a specific time in the day or week for quiet reflection. Just sit and notice what thoughts come to mind.
Professional support	See a therapist, coach, mentor or counselor, or join a specific supportive group for something that resonates for you (e.g. a community group, spiritual practice group or group for people struggling with something you find hard). There are often low-cost, voluntary and online options for professional and group support.
Authentic movement	This is a form of reflection through movement with other people. There are usually movers and witnesses. There are groups all over the world engaged in this practice. Other forms of reflective movement with others that you could explore include 5Rhythms or Open Floor (see end of the book for more resources on all of this).

If you picked one of these to try, reflect on how that was. Did you find it easy or hard to do? What blocks or obstacles did you experience, if any? What did you like about it? What didn't you like? How were you left afterwards? Feel free to adapt and add to the list for what works for you.

One reason that reflective self-care can be helpful is that it gives us a chance to observe our patterns. These are the common habits that we fall into which may be unhelpful for us, hurting us and others in our lives. They are often pretty unconscious, and reflective self-care can help to bring them into consciousness, as well as helping us to understand where they come from. Then we can get more intentional about whether they're serving us or whether they're something we'd like to shift over time.

What we're describing here is the process of many therapies. Therapy is often about helping people to see their patterns and—if they want to—to shift them. Many therapies understand our patterns to be survival strategies that we learned when we were young, but which can be less helpful when we're older. For example, we might have learned to be quiet in order to avoid a family member's aggression, but later in life this stops us from being as confident or outgoing as we'd like to be. We could have become a people-pleaser to prevent us from being bullied at school, but now that's meaning we're not as real as we'd like to be in relationships, and that's getting in the way of intimacy. We may have learned to use coldness or distance to control the people around us, but now we see our loved ones being hurt by that.

Our patterns are never purely individual—something "wrong" with us that needs fixing. Rather, they are embedded within the wider cultures and communities we're part of that teach us how to be. Also, they are often passed on through intergenerational trauma in our family systems, and play out in certain kinds of relationships. Many are social patterns shared by all in a society or community, such as treating certain people as less valuable than ourselves.

Remember this diagram from before? If you're aware of a pattern of yours, write it in the middle and have a go at noting on the diagram the cultural, community and family systems/relationship dynamics this pattern is embedded in.

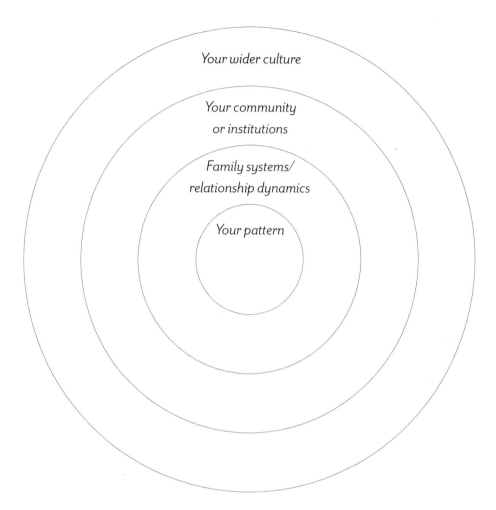

Seeing the embeddedness of our patterns can help lift the sense of blame and responsibility on us as individuals. Sometimes this can actually help us change patterns that are harmful and hurtful to us and those around us. Shame can make us want to hide or run away from these patterns, whereas looking at them with as much curiosity as we can manage may help us make different choices moving forward. We're not destined to repeat unhelpful, hurtful or harmful patterns!

If it is hard to observe your patterns by yourself, then professional or spiritual support, or groups, can be a great idea. Remember that shifting them is a gradual process...

Notice the pattern, do it differently, make that your journey.

As we think about and develop reflective self-care practices that work for us, it might be helpful to also consider our values. Our values often guide our choices and decision-making processes, something that we'll talk about next. Our values are the things we consider important in life. They come both from our own belief systems and from what culture tells us we "should" value. Our individual values and cultural values may or may not map on to one another. If we have complex identities and experiences, we might also feel pulled in different directions by different values from a range of communities.

Let's take some time to sort through our values, then, given that we're focusing on reflective practices in this chapter. This is something that it's worth doing now and again, especially as our values can change over time. For example, we usually don't have the same values at five years old that we have at 20 years old.

There are many lists of values across the internet. You may want to pick one of those by searching for "values list" or you might just want to make your own. Examples of value words include: integrity, honesty, responsibility, care, vitality, fun, freedom, peace. If you're making your own list, we'd recommend coming up with at least 20 words so you have several values to choose from for the next activity.

Once you have your value list, either taken from the internet or self-created, take some time to sort through your values. Which values come from culture and which feel personal? Which ones feel important both culturally and individually? Which are the values that are most important to you? Do they line up with your culture(s) or not? If not, how does that impact you, if at all? Once you pick the ones that are most important to you, you've found you core values. They're your North Star as you journey through life. Group all these core values together.

Now take some time to sort through them and rank them in order of importance. If there are values that are as important as one another, you can group them together. Now consider your core values and their importance in your life. Are they all equally important to each part of you and your life, or are there some that are more important to some parts of you and your life than others? We'll talk more about different parts of ourselves later in this book, but, for now, what we mean is that some values might be more important to the part of you that goes to work every day, for example, rather than your social part.

Once you've done this, think about which values define you. They are the values that make you who you are. They're so important that to let go of these values would feel like a betrayal of yourself. Then write down those values below.

My essential, defining values are...

. . . .

. . . .

. . . .

. . . .

Now that you've figured out what your essential and defining values are, let's talk about making decisions and choices. Don't worry if you have struggled with finding these values. It's also OK to just pick a few values that seem important to you and play with them. You don't have to take all of this super seriously! It's OK to experiment.

Let's consider the way you make decisions and choose what to do. When you look at your essential, defining values, does it seem that they align with the choices you make or not? For example, we may value mutuality in friendships but we find ourselves choosing to see more acquaintances than friends because they keep asking for our time. In this case, we might find that our choices are being driven by outside factors, the squeakiest wheel getting attention, rather than our essential values. Once we notice this, we can try to make more intentional, self-consensual and gentle choices that nourish us and our close relationships.

Take a moment to list some choices you make daily, weekly, monthly and yearly on the page that follows. We have provided some examples in the table. Then highlight or circle the choices you make that are in line with the essential, defining values that you have identified earlier.

Daily	Monthly	Weekly	Yearly
Brushing my teeth	Taking a day to rest	Writing for an hour	Taking time off

Once you have done this, take time to reflect on what happened in the decision-making process for the choices that are not aligned with your values. For example, maybe you keep going to a toxic job every day because of the demands of capitalism. Then take time to consider what factors enabled you to make choices that are in line with your values. What were those factors? Please list them below.

The factors that help me make decisions and choices in line with my essential values are:

. . . .

. . . .

. . . .

. . . .

Many of the reflective self-care practices might seem really focused on our individual experiences, patterns, values and choices. We'll talk more about reflective communal practices towards the end of the book. However, we wanted to mention here that being able to take time for reflective self-care can also help us stay in relationship with one another. If we're coming from a place of reactivity and urgency, we can become more self-focused, even when we're fighting for justice or organizing in community. We might start rushing and forgetting to make everyday choices according to our essential, defining values. For example, we may be part of a labor rights organization that encourages long hours of work without breaks or taking time off sick.

In a way, reflective self-care practices allow us to slow down and be intentional in how we relate to ourselves but also to one another. We're striving here to be in line with disability justice and Indigenous activist frameworks, which foreground interdependence over independence. These practices seem important to us as they enable us to show up in relationships, communities and in the world, with awareness, self-knowledge, coherence and intentionality. We believe that showing up in these ways can help us build and participate in healthier relationships and communities together.

Take a moment right now, for example, to reflect on how your existing or desired reflective self-care practices might help you show up in the way you want to in the relationships and communities you are part of, then note your thoughts in the table below.

Reflective self-care activity	Impact on community/relationships

When we've done reflective self-care, we can become more aware of our patterns, choices and behaviors and their impact on others. It can also be useful here to build in practices of *accountability*: ways in which we will reflect on this impact, take responsibility for it and address it when necessary.

When our behavior has hurt others, wider culture generally encourages us to deny what happened, blame the victim, minimize the impact, claim that we had good intentions and insist that it wasn't part of a wider pattern of behavior. We probably do this to reassure ourselves that we have some control over whether we ourselves are victimized, and that we couldn't possibly be a "bad person." Admitting to impacting others is not about saying we're a bad person or a monster. It's simply acknowledging that we all fall short at times, that this hurts others and that we understand this and want to do better. In fact, if we can start from the assumption that most of the time we all have good intentions, then we can better concentrate on any hurtful or harmful impact, focusing energy and resources appropriately.

If possible, it's great to have a sense of a group of people in your life who you can go to if you are concerned about something you've done or if somebody has brought up something with you. The role of this group would be to help you to reflect on it honestly and kindly, and to take accountability for it if necessary. Similarly, it can be useful to have group support for the times when somebody else's behavior has hurt you.

For situations that are more serious, where people have very different understandings of what happened, or where it's hard to be in contact directly, various—more formal—approaches have been developed. You might like to read about accountability pods, mediation and restorative and transformative justice, for example. Knowing about such things in advance, and having a plan, can help you to pause and put something in place if you do find yourself in this kind of situation (see further resources at the end of the book).

CHAPTER 8

Rituals and Ongoing Practices

Over the last three chapters we've given you lots and lots and lots of ideas for self-care practices of various types that you might build into your life: basic self-care, crisis self-care, kind self-care, just being, reflective self-care and some more community-based forms of self-care. Over the rest of the book there will be even more ideas coming at you.

As we've said, it's definitely not about trying to do All The Things. Rather it's about getting playful and experimenting with what works for you at this point in your life.

Once you have a sense of some forms of self-care you would like to build in, how do you go about doing this?

It can be useful here to think about time. Some self-care practices would be relatively easy to build in every day (e.g. three conscious breaths or a slowed-down cup of tea); others might be a once-a-year or even once-a-decade type thing (e.g. going on a retreat, vacation or workshop).

We find it useful to have a note on our phones of regular self-care practices or routines that we're trying to build in at the following frequencies. MJ's looks something like this, for example:

- *Daily*: morning sit, evening soothing activity, debrief the day before sleep.

- *Weekly*: journal once, see friends at least three times, be in nature at least once.

- *Monthly*: therapy twice, sharing circle twice, moon ritual twice.

- *Seasonally*: rituals around the start of spring, birthday, Halloween and winter solstice.

- *Yearly*: writing retreat with Alex.

We also find it useful to have some sense of the maximum amount of time we'll do social things, work, go on trips at a distance, see clients, and whether these are daily, weekly and so on, to try to avoid overcommitting and overstretching ourselves.

It's important here to balance structure and flexibility. It's good if these kinds of lists can be living documents which can shift as we age, change, transition and learn about new practices and ideas.

Things also happen in our lives which make it hard, if not impossible, to stick to routines. These things can become a lot harder if we're feeling bad about breaking our usual forms of self-care. So it might be useful to also have a sense of the self-care practices that work for us at the following times, and shift into these when they happen:

- Getting sick.

- Traveling.

- Moving home, work or changing/ending a relationship.

- Being in crisis.

- Having someone in our lives needing a lot of care or support.

- Our country or community in upheaval.

We'll include some practices for you to come up with your own rhythms and rituals later in this chapter.

As we just discussed, we'll engage in different self-care practices at various times. The when and how often will change according to what those practices are.

Timing and frequency, however, can also change due to a range of circumstances. For example, we find that when we travel, we're able to keep some practices but not others. Depending where we are and for how long, we might develop new practices, limited to a specific event, such as a writing or spiritual retreat, or we might adapt our usual practices or let go of them completely.

We've already mentioned being in crisis and the importance of WRAP® plans earlier on. However, we might also get sick, have flare-ups of existing disabilities or chronic conditions and so on. We might also face things like sudden loss of a relationship through break-ups or death, loss of a job, not being able to pay our bills, moving and so on. Increasingly, we're also facing environmental crises and challenges.

Even though we've talked about the importance of routines, this is where we remind you that almost nothing in life is a binary, and so, while routines are important, it's almost as important to hold these with flexibility and open hands. What do we mean by this? Holding something with open hands means that we can pick it up or put it down. For example, if we go to the gym three times a week but we get sick or have a flare-up, we can take time to rest and let go of our usual routine until we're ready to pick it up again. This can be incredibly challenging to do in dominant cultures where being sick is almost viewed as a "personal failing." Yet, when we're sick or have a flare-up, our bodies are really telling us to slow down, cancel everything and focus on recuperating and resting. We'll talk more about the importance of listening to our body in Chapter 15.

This can be really difficult if we struggle with all-or-nothing thinking patterns. All-or-nothing patterns can mean we feel it's urgent and important to not change our routines. In fact, we might feel incredibly anxious, to the point of panic, if something changes. However, if we can slow down and come back to our window of tolerance, we might notice that it's OK to change our routine or adapt our self-care practices to the circumstances. Holding our practices with open hands helps us remember that there is a season for everything and sometimes seasons change unexpectedly and independently from our plans. For example, we might have planned to wander and wonder but it's flooding where we live and we need to stay indoors!

What can help us hold our self-care practices with open hands? Curiosity can be an excellent tool in this regard. Asking ourselves, or others, questions engages a different part of the brain and it can help us move away from panic. For example, we might ask ourselves, what's the worst that can happen if we do this instead of that? Or, if our brain is stuck in all-or-nothing thinking—for example, telling us that if we don't sleep eight hours exactly, we'll get sick—we can reply to our brain by saying, well...maybe.

Maybe can be another powerful tool to help us remember that we don't know for certain what will happen. Maybe reminds us that there is a third road—it might be unfamiliar and unknown but it exists. Anything that challenges polarized, all-or-nothing thinking helps us build flexibility and practice, holding ourselves and our practices with open hands.

Now take a moment to think about a time when your plans changed and you felt distressed... What caused the distress? Were you trying to hold on to something too tightly, such as your desire to do something? Were you feeling out of control or helpless? What could have helped in that moment? What did you need to hear, know or remember? Imagine now that you have a time machine and you can travel back to your past self and say and do just the perfect thing. Now note down below what that "perfect thing for you" might be so you can remember it next time your future self is in a similar situation.

. . . .

. . . .

. . . .

Two forms of self-care that many people find helpful are to create a personal altar and to develop a personal ritual which you do fairly regularly. Here are some ideas for how you could do these things.

Make your own altar

We encourage you to find a space where you live to make your altar. If that's not possible, you can make a portable altar, or even a digital one. An altar is just a space—physical or virtual—where you can place objects to symbolize something. You can put whatever you want on this altar. You may want to include pictures or things that are important to you. MJ includes an object representing each side of themselves, for example (see Chapter 18), as well as items representing sea, land and friendship. We have a friend who asks friends to give them items to represent themselves on their altar. You may also want to also include ancestors of blood, spirit, culture or activism. Whatever you include on your altar might be linked to your intention. You may want to start from a specific intention and then build you altar, or just build an altar and then find your intention. It's OK to follow your gut on this one or, if you're part of a specific tradition that already works with altars, you might want to follow this.

Develop your own ritual

Now that you have an altar, you can develop a ritual around it, something to do with your altar regularly. You could decide to spend a little time with your altar every day. It can be just a few minutes. For example, Alex takes a little time with their altar each morning to remember their ancestors, to draw a rune for the day, and to reflect on what's coming up and set an intention for that. When they travel, they make a digital altar on their phone by having images of the deities and ancestors they work with, using a rune app and a digital journal.

You could build a longer ritual around your altar on less frequent occasions. For example, MJ has adapted a Tibetan Buddhist "regret ritual" which takes place on the full and new moon. Each full and new moon (or the nearest free evening), after lighting a candle they spend some time reflecting in their journal on what regrets they've had since the last ritual. They decide what behaviors or habits they'd love to let go of from that period, and what they'd like to bring in for the next couple of weeks. They often represent this letting go and bringing in with tarot cards they have chosen or pictures they have drawn. Sometimes they include a meditation to feel the feelings deeply, as well as expressing gratitude to all the people and places—inside and out—who support them.

You can weave together whatever forms of self-care you like into a ritual that works for you.

You might be having some thoughts about cultural appropriation here. That's good. We'd like to invite you to think about the relationship you have with ideas such as altars or rituals. You may have rituals and altar-making traditions already, or you might not. We choose rituals that make sense to us given our own spiritual paths.

Whatever you choose, you can be slow and intentional. Are you reclaiming a practice initially lost to you through the impact of ongoing settler-colonial violence? Are you building a relationship with a spiritual tradition that is not from your culture? If so, is it a tradition open to people of other cultures? Who are you learning from? Who are your elders and teachers? Why are you making the choices you are making? We invite you to engage some of the reflective practices already discussed, together with accountability to communities and traditions you might be engaging with.

It's also OK to make up your own altars and rituals if you want to engage with those ideas in a more secular context. For example, brushing our teeth can be considered a ritual, even though it's not a spiritual ritual. We might think of a work desk or a kitchen as an altar where we do meaningful work. Whatever you choose, we hope you can be intentional, transparent and accountable with your choices.

On the following pages, think for yourself about what daily, weekly and monthly self-care practices you would like to build into your life. Try to think realistically about what will fit in with your existing everyday life, or what you would stop doing in order to make that time. It's also good to think about balancing different forms of self-care. For example:

Kind/Reflective

Alone/With others

Being/Doing

Still/Moving

Ones I find easy/Ones I find more challenging

Online/Offline

Ones I build in regularly/Ones I do on the spot if things get hard

Daily self-care practices

. . . .

. . . .

. . . .

. . . .

. . . .

. . . .

. . . .

Weekly self-care practices

. . . .

. . . .

. . . .

. . . .

. . . .

. . . .

. . . .

Monthly self-care practices

. . . .

. . . .

. . . .

. . . .

. . . .

. . . .

On this page, think for yourself about what seasonal and yearly self-care practices or rituals you would like to build into your life. Try to think realistically about what will fit in with your existing everyday life, or what you would stop doing in order to make that time. It's also good to think about balancing different forms of self-care as mentioned on the previous page.

Examples of things you might consider on this page include how you celebrate the turning of the years/seasons, anniversaries and birthdays, holidays, festivals and retreats, and how you engage with dominant culture holidays and rituals relating to your faith or spirituality.

Seasonal self-care practices

. . . .

. . . .

. . . .

. . . .

. . . .

. . . .

. . . .

Yearly self-care practices

. . . .

. . . .

. . . .

. . . .

. . . .

. . . .

. . . .

We'll come back to self-care planning in more detail towards the end of the book, but we hope this gives you something to start playing with.

M.Y.O. Slow Down Page

Your chosen activity, for this moment, here.

Staying With Feelings

CHAPTER 9

Why Are Emotions Important?

Back in the 1960s, the humanistic therapist Eugene Gendlin studied the differences between people whose lives improved after counseling and those who didn't feel any better. Listening to many recordings of therapy sessions, he noticed that the clients helped by therapy did something that the other clients didn't do. This was a kind of checking in where they slowed down, tuned in to themselves and reported what they were experiencing, often explaining how they were feeling in their bodies and trying to find the best words to describe their emotional experience.

Gendlin went on to develop *focusing* as a practice for people to learn how to stay with their feelings like this. We'll describe how to do this in a moment. However, it's telling that many different forms of psychotherapy and spiritual traditions have developed similar practices which involve slowing down and tuning in to our emotions. The current popularity of *mindfulness* shows just how much this kind of approach seems to resonate with people.

This chapter is all about why it's an important part of self-care to cultivate the capacity to stay with our feelings, and how we can go about doing that. We hope that as you work through the chapter, it will help you figure out your own emotional landscape: which feelings you tend to prefer and which you tend to avoid. It'll also give you several possible practices for learning to stay with your feelings. As always, different things work for different people, so it's all about figuring out what works best for you. Please note that in this workbook we're using the words "feelings" and "emotions" interchangeably.

These kinds of practices are important because during our lives we generally learn the opposite to staying with feelings: we're encouraged to shut off or eradicate some kinds of emotional experiences and to strive for or fixate on others. This can limit us in all kinds of ways. We often try to avoid situations and people that give us "negative feelings," and grasp too tightly those which give us "positive" ones. When emotions do bubble up—as they inevitably will—we often attempt to deny or suppress some of them and to fake or force others. This can mean that only certain sides of ourselves develop, and it often gives a false impression to people in our lives, which then interferes with our relationships.

Shutting off from our feelings—or avoiding them—is a problem because emotions are often trying to give us important information. For example, fear may be telling us a situation is not safe enough; anger that we need to hold our boundaries; and sadness that it's time to grieve. When we're in good contact and communication with our feelings, we're better able to hang out with them, listen to the messages they have for us and distinguish when they are providing us with urgent information about the present and when they are coming up because the present is reminding us about the past. However, it's important to remember that while emotions are information, they're not facts.

For example, if we have experienced trauma, our emotions might be more about the past than the present. It can be useful to check in with a number of trusted people around us when we're not sure if our emotions are in line with what's happening in the present or not.

Enough preamble. Let's get to know your feelings...

The Pixar movie *Inside Out* is one of the best introductions to how emotions work and what happens when we try to avoid or suppress some of them. We'd highly recommend watching the film, although we don't condone the moments of casual fatphobia and sexism. Here's an overview of the plot...

The film follows an 11-year-old, Riley, and her emotions—Joy, Sadness, Disgust, Anger and Fear—as her family move city. Previously, Riley's inner world was dominated by Joy who made it her business to ensure that Riley remained as happy as possible, building up a store of mostly joyful memories which have, in turn, shaped her personality. However, following the move, many of these memories become "tainted" by Sadness, who can't seem to stop herself from touching them and turning them blue.

In her attempts to prevent Sadness from causing any more damage, Joy manages to get both of them ejected from the control room to the outer reaches of Riley's inner world. This leaves Anger, Fear and Disgust in charge while Joy and Sadness try everything they can to get back before Riley runs away from her new home. We see how Riley and Joy's attempts to keep her joyful tragically have the opposite effect. By trying to sustain her joyful persona in the face of great pain, she actually becomes angry, anxious and cut-off, and risks losing the love of her parents as they don't recognize her anymore.

The message of *Inside Out* is that we need all of our emotions, not just the so-called "good" or "positive" ones. Things work pretty badly when just one of the emotions takes charge, and much better when they all work together through being equally valued.

Think about the feelings that you're familiar with. Have a go at sketching them here. You could draw them like the characters in *Inside Out*, or just use colors or shapes that feel right for you. You might want to draw them bigger and smaller, or more central and further away, to depict how familiar you are with them, or how much you tend to experience them.

Sometimes the desire to divide emotions into good or bad can emerge from our fear of distressing emotions. If, for some reason, we have not built capacity to tolerate emotional distress, "big" emotions such as anger can feel overwhelming. We'll talk in a moment about all the ways in which we might try to suppress emotions. For now, though, we want to stay with why it's a bad idea to suppress some emotions.

Often the desire is to experience only "feel-good" emotions and move away from the bad, overwhelming or distressing ones. Unfortunately, as we'll discuss in more depth on the next page, this doesn't work. Let's take a moment to consider which emotions we feel more or less comfortable with. Consider the feelings wheel below. At the center are our most basic emotions, similar to the movie *Inside Out* mentioned earlier, then those feelings are broken down in more nuanced ways as the wheel moves out and becomes larger. Take your time and circle or annotate which feelings you're not comfortable with or even find to be distressing or overwhelming.

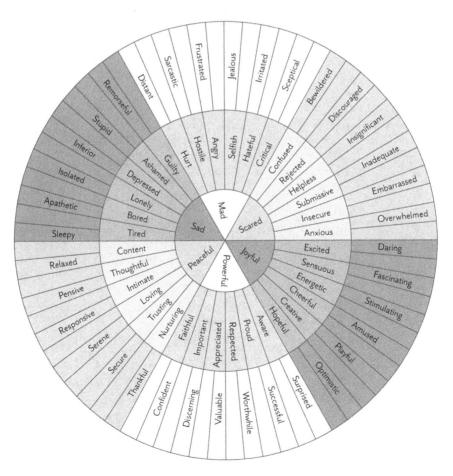

Now that you've considered what feelings you're not as comfortable with, or even find overwhelming and distressing, let's think about all the ways in which we might try to suppress those feelings, both in our everyday lives and at times of crisis.

Some common suppressing strategies when feeling "too emotional or distressed" are: eating, smoking, drinking alcohol, watching a lot of TV, getting lost in a book, using substances (including taking too many painkillers), having sex, surrounding ourselves with noise and/or people, isolating ourselves, meditating in a dissociative way (e.g. not being present but getting lost in our own head and/or fantasies), fantasizing, creating a story that's different from what happened (especially if we can't tolerate the feelings we have about our own behaviors), moving/traveling a lot. **Note:** we're not saying here that any of these things are "bad" to do in general. Many of them can be great forms of self-care at times! As we've said before, it's not about *what* you're doing, more about *why* and *how* you're doing it.

The last strategy really highlights how when we're trying to suppress feelings that are somehow intolerable, we're literally trying to get away from ourselves! Unfortunately, as a famous phrase with an unclear origin states, "Wherever you go, there you are."

Suppressing our emotions, though, is not just unhelpful because they will eventually resurface in some way, shape or form, but also because we cannot suppress the unwanted emotions without also suppressing our capacity to feel joy, connection and pleasure. We might be able to feel the "good" without the "bad" for a short period of time but, eventually, we lose our capacity to feel our own aliveness and to authentically connect with others, if we keep trying to suppress certain emotions.

We all try to get away from negative emotions from time to time and, sometimes, this is even necessary. For example, if we struggle with suicidality, complex post-traumatic stress disorder (PTSD), depression and other conditions that lead us to spiral into negative emotions, we might need to move away from those, and we'll talk about this a little bit more later. Right now, let's reflect on all the ways in which you might suppress those emotions that you've already identified as being uncomfortable, overwhelming or distressing. You can list your strategies for suppressing emotions on the next page, draw them or create a mind map.

These are all the different ways in which I suppress emotions I find intolerable...

Existential therapist Emmy van Deurzen came up with this compass of emotions (2008). She imagines the emotions on a wheel which we travel around all of the time, moving from "high" feelings such as joy and pride, through anger and fear to "low" feelings such as sadness, and then up the other side through envy and hope to joy again.

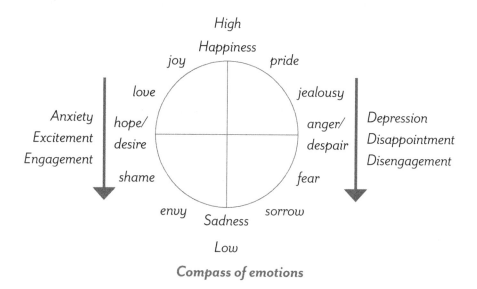

Compass of emotions

Importantly, Emmy van Deurzen argues that we need to be able to experience all of the emotions to go around the compass like this. If there are emotions that we shut down or avoid, then we're likely to get stuck in one place. Paradoxically, if we disallow one emotion—such as sadness—we're likely to get stuck and find that we stop experiencing other emotions—such as joy—too. If we lose the capacity to experience some of the emotions entirely, we risk falling into depression and all of our emotions becoming shut off.

Reflect on the compass for a minute. Which parts of it do you find yourself spending a lot of time in? Which parts not so much? Where, if anywhere, do you tend to get stuck?

It may not be that we always move in the same direction on the compass, or that certain emotions always follow others. Indeed, we can often experience seemingly opposing emotions at the same time (joy and sadness, anger and hope, fear and determination).

There's something important here about developing the ability to stay with all of the different consecutive or simultaneous aspects of our emotional experience, rather than emphasizing just one part of it. For example, when we're making a decision, we can stay with both the feelings that draw us towards something and those that push us away from it.

Existential therapists regard all feelings as sensible responses that have something to tell us, as long as we're up for listening to them.

CHAPTER 10

Your Relationship With Feelings

The problem is that, through our lives, most of us learn that certain emotions are not acceptable: either to express or, often, even to experience. We may also learn that certain feelings are important, or that we should be expressing all of our feelings all of the time.

You might think back to moments in your own childhood and adolescence when you learned that certain feelings were acceptable and unacceptable. Or perhaps as an adult, you found that particular emotions weren't allowed—or were expected—in certain relationships or in the workplace. These lessons are learned at different times—and around different emotions—for each of us, and it can be gradual or sudden, or both. You might want to reflect on what avoiding or expressing those emotions meant for how you related to yourself, other people and your life more widely.

Where do these messages about feelings come from? We can see it on multiple levels. Remember the diagram on the next page? We'll work through this for feelings on the following pages. Importantly here, each level of the diagram can reinforce and resist the messages we get at the other levels. For example, we might get the same sense of the emotions that it is "good" to feel or express at all levels of culture, community and relationships, or we might get different messages at different levels.

The world and your
wider culture

Your community
or institutions

Your close
relationships

Within
yourself

On the outer level, our wider culture gives us strong messages about which emotions it is OK to express or feel and which it isn't. Generally, in dominant Anglo culture, we're encouraged to express happiness and "positive" experiences and not "negative" ones. The British "stiff upper lip" discourages expressions of fear, and perhaps anger, for example. Alternatively, Italians tend to be pretty expressive, to the point that holding individual boundaries around emotions can be challenging. Also, messages differ depending on our individual identities, with certain emotions being seen as more or less acceptable for people of certain genders, classes, ages or nationalities, for example.

Think about the world around you and your own wider culture. What messages do you receive there about what emotions are acceptable—and unacceptable—for a person like you to feel and/or express? You might like to write, draw or paste in illustrations of these messages on the diagram on the next page. If you like, you can do this on one side of the page for the messages you received growing up, and on the other side of the page for the ones that are around you now.

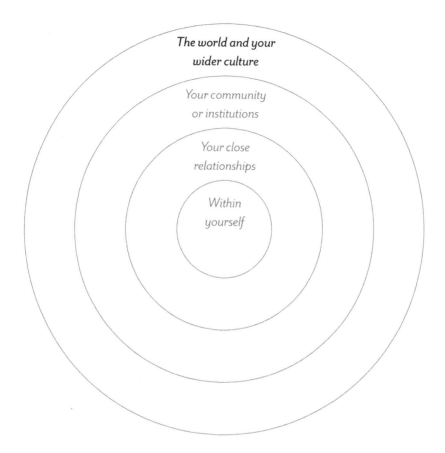

On the next level in, our communities and institutions also reinforce many of these messages. For example, in school we might have been judged for being too enthusiastic or too quiet. In the workplace, there might be no place for "becoming emotional," or we might be encouraged to look as if we're all in a constant state of anxiety, with overwhelming feelings. We might have community norms about whether it's good or bad to express anger or jealousy.

It's easy to find ourselves joining in a kind of tone policing in our communities—of whatever kind—whereby certain emotions are deemed unacceptable to admit to or express, for certain people or across the board. It's worth being mindful of this whenever we find ourselves judging how somebody "should" or "shouldn't" feel about something.

Think about your own communities and institutions. What messages do you receive there about what emotions are acceptable—and unacceptable—to feel and/or express? You might like to write, draw or paste in illustrations of these messages on the diagram on the next page. If you like, you can do this on one side of the page for the messages you received growing up, and on the other side of the page for the ones that are around you now.

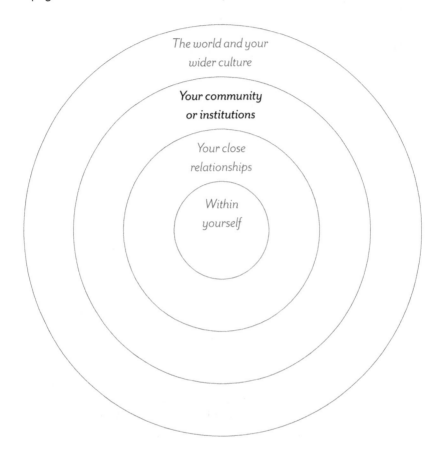

At the level of our close relationships, we learn a great deal about acceptable and unacceptable feelings from family and friends around us. It's important to remember that other close people in our lives often live in the same wider culture as we do, with all of its crappy messages about acceptable and unacceptable feelings. They're also part of institutions and communities that might have had a deep impact on them. And they're part of their own family systems wherein certain emotions may have been deemed vital or too dangerous or threatening. So they may well respond by giving us messages that our fear, sadness, anger, joy, disgust or other feelings are not something that they can be around, that they can't love us if we express them, or that we should protect them from those feelings.

Systemic therapy also talks about how people in family and friendship groups often become scapegoated in relation to certain feelings—for example, as "the happy one," "the problem one," the person who has to worry about everybody, or the person who everyone is scared of upsetting. The system as a whole can keep us stuck there. This means that other people don't have to deal with their own uncomfortable feelings if someone else in the family or group is "the problem."

Think about your own close relationships. What messages do you receive there about what emotions are acceptable—and unacceptable—to feel and/or express? You might like to write, draw or paste in illustrations of these messages on the diagram below. If you like, you can do this on one side of the page for the messages you received growing up, and on the other side of the page for the ones that are around you now.

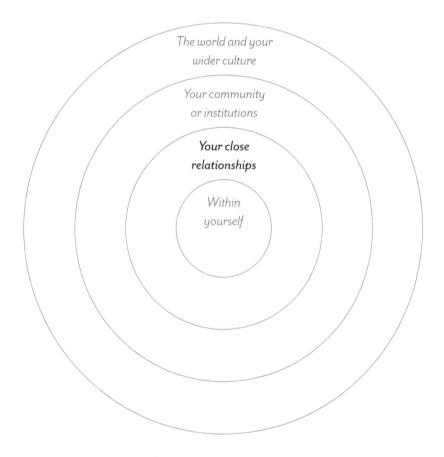

We will have internalized all of these messages from the other levels. Either we'll have managed to find a way of shutting down the "bad" emotions entirely, or, perhaps, in trying to shut them down we'll have managed to make them shout more loudly, so that we become easily emotionally flooded or overwhelm others with our emotions. There are so many ways that this can go.

Think about your own inner landscape. What messages do you give yourself about what emotions are acceptable—and unacceptable—to feel and/or express? You might like to write, draw or paste in illustrations of these messages on the diagram below. If you like, you can do this on one side of the page for the messages you received growing up, and on the other side of the page for the ones that are around you now.

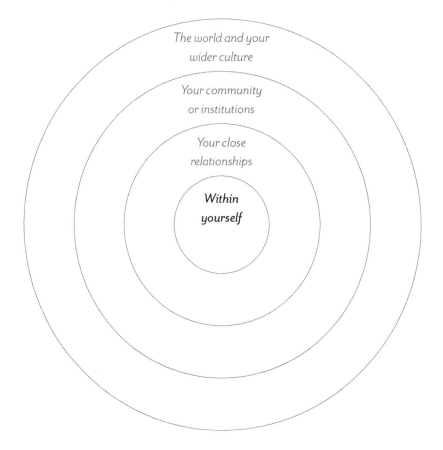

Now you might like to reflect on what working through these levels was like for you. What have you learned about your relationship with your emotions? What are the key messages you received about feelings in the past, and today? How do you relate to those messages? How would you like to relate to them?

CHAPTER 11

How to Stay With Your Feelings

The important question is what can we do now? Here we are with all these imbalances, exaggerations and silences in our emotional states. What can we do about it?

The answer that many different therapies and spiritual traditions have come up with is the idea of staying with our feelings. We'll describe a couple of these practices: a Buddhist approach called "FEAR," and Gendlin's humanistic therapy practice of focusing (1982). There are several similar practices if these don't work for you, and several different versions of these ones as well. Many of the self-care practices that we've already covered elsewhere in the book can be adapted for staying with feelings—for example, journaling about how we're feeling, going for a walk to feel a feeling, drawing the feeling, finding music that fits our mood and dancing the feeling.

Remember again that different things work for different people, and at different times in their lives. For example, some people like practices where you sit quietly and meditate alone. Others much prefer to talk it through with another person. Some like to work things through in writing or drawing. For some people, bodily movement is vital to help the feelings move too.

Of course, given how many years most of us have spent suppressing or being flooded by certain emotions, it can take a long time to open up this kind of line of communication. Practices like this can feel very unfamiliar at first and it can take a while to get the hang of them.

Before we describe the two practices for staying with feelings, it's vital to say something about when to do this kind of practice, and when not to.

We've already talked in Chapter 9 about suppressing feelings—the tendency a lot of us have to move away from feelings as soon as they come up, particularly intense feelings. However, there's a risk that learning about staying with feelings can make us do the opposite, assuming that the "right" thing to do is always to move towards them.

Actually, from a trauma-informed perspective, it's sometimes unwise to go towards feelings—or stay with them—when we're overwhelmed or reactive, or when the feelings are very intense. Certainly, it's not a great idea when we're in the midst of an intense trauma response. The reason for this is that it's easy to re-traumatize ourselves, or further overwhelm ourselves—for example, if we push ourselves into remembering extremely painful things before we are ready, or push ourselves to remain in a state of panic or deep grief in order to "feel the feeling."

So, when is it a good idea to stay with feelings and when not? Our friend Sophia Graham, who writes the *Love Uncommon* blog, came up with this simple suggestion. She says:

I find the simple 1–10 scale of emotional activation really helpful. I notice my overall emotional activation, irrespective of which emotions I'm feeling, and rate that on a 1–10 scale, with 1 being lowest intensity and 10 being completely overwhelmed. That means just checking in with my body about my current level of emotional activation.

How intense are my emotions in this moment?

1   2   3   4   5   6   7   8   9   10

You might like to have a go at this for how you're feeling right now. What about the last time you felt a big feeling?

Sophia suggests that if our feelings are in the 4–7 range, then we might be in a really good place for practicing staying with feelings. If we're in 1–3, then we might benefit from tuning into what feelings might be there. If we're in 8–10, then it's much more about self-care and self-soothing: bringing ourselves back to a safer, less intense place. Please note that these numbers are subjective and you might want to figure out your own tolerable range. You might like to keep a list of the soothing practices that work for you under those circumstances. We mentioned some of these in Chapter 5 when we wrote about trauma. A really important part of trauma work is noticing when we're activated and feeling unsafe, and being able to take ourselves out of the situation and prioritize taking care of ourselves, rather than forcing ourselves to stay.

Sometimes we're able to do the kinds of practices we're talking about here "on the spot" when we're having a feeling. At other times, that is too hard and it's better to wait until we're feeling calm and then work with the memory of the feeling. That is just fine. For most of us, it's a good idea to build up gradually from the emotions that we find easier and less loaded, to the ones that are particularly difficult for us based on our histories. It can also be great to get support from a trauma-informed professional to work with the more challenging feelings.

Buddhist teacher Pema Chödrön (2010) provides a simple practice for staying with feelings using the acronym FEAR (although it is useful for any emotion, not just fear!):

Find the feeling in your body.

Embrace it (instead of trying to get rid of it, or distracting yourself from it).

Allow thoughts about it to dissolve, and abide with the feeling.

Remember all of the other people who feel, and have felt, this way.

Finding the feeling in your body is about noticing the sensations that you're having: a tight throat, a churning belly or a sense of emptiness, for example. We'll say more about how to do this in the next pages.

Embracing the feeling is about just letting it be there without trying to get rid of it or label it.

Pema talks about how we often get caught up in a storyline about feelings. For example: "Oh no, I'm feeling low. What's going on? Maybe I'm falling into depression. What's wrong with me? Everything's going well—I shouldn't feel depressed. It's stupid to be feeling like this. I'm so fed up with myself. Other people have far worse things going on than I do." And so on, and so on.

Allowing the thoughts to dissolve is about letting go of these storylines and just remaining with the actual feeling: its texture, strength, color, where you feel it in your body, the sensation.

It can also be really helpful to *remember* to use tough feelings as a way of connecting with all the other people who're feeling this way. This turns you outwards towards the world, develops compassion and can leave you feeling less alone. Remembering others can be particularly helpful if we're stuck in a trauma response (one of the four Fs). Trauma tends to make us self-focused, so remembering that others can have similar experiences to us and have their own suffering can help us move whatever feelings we're stuck in more easily.

Feelings about feelings

Because we receive such limiting messages about emotions from our wider culture, communities and relationships growing up, people often notice in practices like these that feelings about feelings come up. For example, you might start with a fluttery, frightened feeling and then quickly find that a hot, angry feeling comes up about that feeling. Or you might start with a clenched, tense feeling and, as you explore it, realize that there's an empty, sad feeling underneath it.

Buddhists refer to feelings about feelings as the "second arrow." It's as if we're hit by one arrow (the feeling) and then another one (the feeling about the feeling). For example, if we've been taught to protect other people from our sadness, any sad feelings are likely to be followed by a wave of guilt or shame.

Learning to stay with our feelings often helps us to remain with the first feeling that comes up without all of those second arrows. On their own, the first arrow feelings are often a lot less overwhelming. If second arrow feelings do come up when we're staying with feelings, it's good to stay with them too: "I notice I'm feeling angry," "I notice I'm feeling disgusted at myself for being angry," "I notice I'm feeling sad about how quickly I feel self-disgust" and so on. All of the feelings are OK. You can stay with all of them or, if you're feeling overwhelmed, it's always OK to stop and go do something else.

Try the FEAR practice now—or later—and reflect on how you found it.

. . . .

. . . .

. . . .

. . . .

Focusing is a practice for giving kind attention to each of our feelings, whenever any of them are wanting our attention. The most basic form of focusing goes like this:

Arriving: Sit comfortably and quietly and bring your attention slowly to your body and how it's feeling.

Meeting: Ask what wants your attention. Focus in on any sensation or "felt sense" that you notice in your body (e.g. a tightness of the throat, a clenched stomach or an emptiness). Say "hello" to that sensation: welcome it warmly. Check in with yourself whether it feels OK to spend some time on that sensation now (if not, it's fine to stop, or to focus on something different).

Being with: Really attend to the sensation, try to find the best way to describe it (e.g. it's like a dense ball stuck in my throat). Check back in with the sensation to see whether that description fits well enough, or whether you need to change it or add to it (e.g. it's not just stuck, it's as if it's rammed in there, like a cork in a bottle).

Stay with the feeling, with interested curiosity, not trying to change it or to force it to communicate, just being with it gently and curiously. Try to understand it from its point of view. Notice any words, images, memories or metaphors that come to mind. Acknowledge everything that comes up, such as further feelings or lack of feelings.

Closing: When it feels ready to finish, you can check in whether there's anything more that wants your attention. If not, express gratitude to the feeling, and to your body, and reassure it that you'll keep coming back to listen to it—and other feelings—in this friendly way.

You can do the focusing practice on your own as a kind of meditation, either learning it and taking yourself through it with your eyes closed, or reading through each bullet point in time and reflecting on it, perhaps noting down what comes to you on a piece of paper.

Try focusing practice now—or later—and reflect on how you found it.

. . . .

. . . .

. . . .

. . . .

Many people find the support of another person very helpful for focusing practice. There are formal therapists and focusing groups, or you can get together with a friend and take each other through it. Obviously, it needs to be somebody whom you trust and feel safe enough with.

Being the "listener" with somebody who is doing focusing is only about being with them and listening: it doesn't require special skills or knowledge. You don't drive the focusing, but rather they talk themselves through the stages (although you can remind them if they've forgotten what's next).

When listening to somebody who is taking themselves through focusing, this is what you need to do:

- Sit comfortably and quietly opposite the other person, trying to be present with them, and with your own body, feelings and responses.

- Let them know how much time they have (perhaps 10–15 minutes).

- Wait till they speak and then make sure you pause before responding, often just with minimal prompts (mm, yes, uh-uh, etc.).

- Reflect back what they've said, using the same words that they've used to describe the emotions, bodily sensations or images that have come up for them. If they say a lot of things, just reflect back the last thing.

- Let them know when they're reaching the end of the time so that they can move towards the ending.

Don't ask questions, interpret or analyze what they're saying, or give suggestions or advice.

Another approach to focusing, instead of starting from the bodily sensation, is to start by asking what calls for attention in your life at the moment. You can start from a specific recent memory and take yourself through the same questions in relation to that.

You might find it useful to consider all these four elements listed below while focusing on a particular memory. During or afterwards, you could note down anything that comes up in these categories, or draw them as pictures or abstract colors and shapes.

- *Bodily sensations*: Where do you feel it in your body and how does it feel?

- *Symbols and images*: What images pop into your mind? What fantasies or metaphors?

- *Emotional qualities*: What's the emotional feeling? What words best describe it?

- *Life connections*: What things in your life, past and present, do you find yourself connecting with? Does the recent memory remind you of earlier memories?

Try a focusing partnership, or focusing on a memory, now—or later—and reflect on how you found it.

. . . .

. . . .

. . . .

. . . .

CHAPTER 12

Finding Presence

We've talked about slowing down and being present in Chapters 4 and 6. Then we've also introduced you to some practices for being present with feelings in Chapter 11. You'll find that we keep coming back to presence quite a bit in this book. This is because when we're present in the here and now, we're much more capable of taking care of ourselves and one another in healthy, relationship-building ways.

Unfortunately, many dominant Anglo cultures are all about fast and busy, rather than slow and engaged. This means that instead of staying with our feelings, our tendency might be rushing to react, usually by "solving" or "fixing" them in some way, or to withdraw from them or suppress them, as discussed earlier. This is another way in which all-or-nothing patterns manifest: we want either to feel resolved in some way or to get away from the feelings completely. This means that instead of being with what is and taking care of ourselves in that moment, we're trying to rush somewhere else, bypassing any care which might need tending to for us and those around us, in the present. Let's look at those two tendencies in our own lives for a moment.

Reacting

Examples of reacting or rushing to "solve" or "fix" emotional issues might be: responding immediately to a challenging email, lashing out at someone who has upset us, or making a snap decision about a difficult situation. Have you ever done any of those things? What does reacting look like for you? Take a moment to notice when you might have come from a place of reactivity in response to emotions and/or situations...

Then take a moment to notice the impact of your reaction. Have you ever felt as if maybe you would have dealt with the situation differently if you had waited an hour or two, or even a day or a week? Have you ever felt as if the problem and feelings got bigger instead of being "resolved"? What might have been possible if you had waited?

Withdrawing

Examples of withdrawing might be: waking up with unresolved feelings, or even just anxious and irritated and rushing to work instead of paying attention to those feelings; feeling troubled by something at the end of the day but getting lost in watching TV or socializing instead of being present with those feelings. Have you ever done any of those things? What does withdrawing look like for you? Take a moment to notice when you might have come from a place of withdrawing and avoiding in response to emotions and/or situations...

. . . .

. . . .

. . . .

. . . .

Then take a moment to notice the impact of your withdrawal/avoidance. Did you feel isolated and alone with your feelings? Have you ever felt as if the feelings got bigger instead of "going away"? What might have been possible if you had stayed with your feelings?

. . . .

. . . .

. . . .

. . . .

An alternative to withdrawing or reacting is to slow down and stay with the original feelings. This can be called *refraining* or *pausing*.

We talked about *refraining* or *pausing* as an alternative to reacting or avoiding and withdrawing. Another option, this one from psychologist Alan Marlatt, can be called *urge surfing* (Marlatt and Gordon 1985). In mindfulness, sometimes this is also called *riding the waves*. No matter what we call them, in many ways those alternatives to either immediately reacting or avoiding and withdrawing are all about impulse control. Our instincts are either to dive in, head first, no questions asked, or to run away. Remember those survival/trauma responses? Doesn't this sound a lot like fight or flight?

If we feel a sense of urgency and, as one of our teachers, Kathy Kain, said to us, "there's no fire, blood or flood," then there is no factual emergency. The reality is that we can pause. Is anyone going to die if you don't respond to that email immediately? Is anything on fire in front of you? Is there a need to respond immediately or run away (not an internal feeling or impulse but an objective need)? If the answer is no, it means it's likely not an urgent crisis, but it might feel like one for us because of all-or-nothing patterns.

This might seem counter to what we stated earlier that emotions are information. The challenge is that our emotions can get tangled in the past and in our trauma histories. This means that while emotions are information, we do not necessarily need to dive into or run away from them immediately.

This is where *refraining*, *pausing*, *urge surfing*, *riding the waves*, or *simply staying with what is* without taking immediate action come in. In order to do this, though, we need to be able to start differentiating between what feels internally uncomfortable, and even intolerable at times, and what is an actual crisis that requires an immediate response (spoiler alert: not many things are urgent crises that require an immediate response in our everyday lives). If we have a history of trauma, this can be challenging to do and it's OK to get support from trusted professionals, spiritual counselors, peers or whatever support network you have or want to connect with.

So, how can we pause if we're not used to it? The secret is not rushing towards the impulse we're feeling. Rather, we notice it and we sit with it. If this does not feel tolerable, it's OK. This is a skill that needs to be built patiently, over time, and that often requires external support for many of us.

If you want to try it out, here's an activity. Think about a situation that is mildly uncomfortable, *not* distressing, just something that makes you squirm lightly. Bring that situation to mind as vividly as possible and notice whether that uncomfortable feeling re-emerges. As you do this, set a timer for 20 minutes and just sit and notice what's happening in that time. You might want to journal if just sitting feels like too much, or take a slow and gentle walk, or move slowly as you notice the emotions rise and fall. When the timer goes off, notice whether the emotions still feel as uncomfortable or not. Are they as intense as they were at the beginning of the exercise? Most intense emotions cannot be sustained by our nervous system for a long time. We tend to rise and then fall, and usually 20–30 minutes is about the length of time that big emotions or strong urges last.

You can also search the internet for *urge surfing* as there are videos and meditation techniques to help with this. **Note:** If emotions feel intolerable and you want to hurt yourself or someone else, please use the five colors, four shapes, three textures, two sounds, one taste or smell, or any other grounding and/or distracting technique you need to keep yourself and others safe.

OK, so we've noticed our urge to rush in and react or avoid and withdraw, and we thought about pausing, refraining and urge surfing, so now what? This is the presence, the "stillness" that Naomi Ortiz talks about in the quote we used earlier. In that pause between feeling and acting is *presence*.

Elsewhere in her book, *Sustaining Spirit: Self-Care for Social Justice* (2018, p.39), Naomi writes:

Nourishment follows by feeling emotions and listening to what these sensations tell me. Just by noticing this information, even something as simple as how the sun feels on my skin, I'm practicing noticing what nourishes me and what does not. Through this critical-feeling, I begin to understand what my needs might be.

It's here, in *presence* with ourselves, our feelings, emotions, sensations, the whole of what is in this moment, that we can find what we need, if we can pause and not rush. This is the place where we learn who we are and also what we need to sustain ourselves. This is the place where we can build relationship with ourselves and our needs, but also with the world around us. In this place, we can make connections with our thinking and feeling patterns. Do they come from the past? Are they about the present situation, or both? When we slow down, pause and are present with ourselves, we can start untangling the threads that often keep us tethered to our pain from the past and to fear of pain in the future.

Enough talking about *presence* for now. Let's try to experience it. What are the moments in which you can find flow in the present. It can be anything: sitting, walking, washing the dishes, petting an animal, holding a trusted friend's hand, praying, hugging a tree, lighting a candle to an ancestor. What helps you stay in the present moment, right here and now, even if for a few seconds? Take a few moments to think about this, or get in touch with *presence*.

Right here, right now.

When we can be present with ourselves and our feelings, we can also be more present with others and their feelings. This is because we might respond to the feelings in other people in a way that's similar to how we respond to ourselves. Do we find anger really uncomfortable in ourselves? We're likely not to be able to tolerate this in others either. Do we find slowing down intolerable? We probably resent people who go "too slow" in our lives.

This means that often we're reacting to other people's feelings by rushing in to "fix" or "solve" them, just as we might do with our own. Or we might blame, shame or avoid others because of their feelings. Being around other people's feelings impacts us because we're co-regulating beings. This means that if people around us feel anxious, we might notice our own heart beat faster and so on. Part of being able to pause and cultivate presence is also about learning to distinguish between our own and other people's feelings.

When we can separate our own feelings from other people's, it becomes easier to both take responsibility for our own feelings and to be present with others, even when they're having "big" emotions that we might have previously found hard to be around. Paradoxically, when we recognize our connection, and that we do impact each other, we're also more able to distinguish the boundaries between us and know where we and our feelings end, and the other and their feelings begin.

For example, if we have had a role in somebody else's pain, then we may be able to bear the guilt of that fact, rather than becoming overwhelmed and requiring them—and others—to take care of us, instead of focusing on them and their pain. Part of this is being able to recognize the imperfect and problematic aspects of ourselves—or, as we like to call it, our humanity—and the limitations in what we can offer, rather than trying to project an image of a perfect person who keeps everyone happy (remember, that would be fawning, another traumatic/survival response).

Now take a moment to think about people whom you find it easy or challenging to be around. Who are they? When do you enjoy being around them and when do you find it difficult? Are there certain feelings in other people that make you want to run away or move close to them? What are they? It's also OK to notice that you might not feel safe around certain people. Do you have an idea of why that might be the case? What is it about them that feels unsafe for you? We don't have to stay in relationship with everybody at all times! Take time to note your reflections on the next page in any way that feels good to you.

. . . .

. . . .

. . . .

. . . .

. . . .

. . . .

. . . .

. . . .

. . . .

If you find yourself merging with other people—that is, you don't know where you end and they begin—you may want to try imagining a bubble of one color around you and a bubble of a different color around them. This can help us differentiate between our own nervous system and that of the other person, by creating a boundary between us. This can help us ground in our own feelings again.

Cultivating presence does not mean that we're going to become some sort of enlightened being who is never going to feel distress again, and who is perfect at relationships! We just wanted to be very clear on that. Cultivating and finding presence is the practice of a lifetime. It's a practice because so many things pull us away from presence: a bird flying by, a change in the weather, a friend's email, our own feelings and bodies. It's human to not be able to live in presence 100 percent—or even 10 percent—of the time.

However, we can cultivate, find and nurture presence in our everyday lives. We'd like to invite you to spend a day noticing and cultivating presence. Then come back and note in words, drawing, colors or a mind map what you've learned.

M.Y.O. Slow Down Page

Remember, this is your space...

Somatic Self-Care

CHAPTER 13

∞

Why Is the Body Important?

Different cultures, as well as different spiritual and religious traditions, have a range of beliefs when it comes to bodies. In many Anglo and Western dominant cultures, there seems to have been a split between mind and body, at least since French philosopher and mathematician René Descartes came up with his famous "I think, therefore I am" in the 1600s. It could be argued that this split is also promoted in Plato's ideas about a singular genuine knowledge and the value he attributed to rational thought. Regardless of who we attribute the mind/body split to, this seems to be a dominant paradigm in Anglo and Western thinking. Not all cultures believe this, of course.

Many Buddhist philosophers have highlighted that there is no separation between self and other, let alone between mind and body. Several Eastern cultures seem to have similar views, in which the body is not separate from the mind. For example, Chinese medicine views the whole person as a system and delivers treatment according to this. No matter which culture we consider, philosophers and spiritual leaders have been thinking about the mind and body and their connections for a long time.

Many Indigenous cultures across the globe also do not view body and mind as separate but rather as part of a whole. For example, Naomi Ortiz (2018) talks about critical feeling in her book. One of Alex's beloved queer siblings and elders, Donald Engstrom-Reese, who is Sami, has often highlighted to us how talking about the body as separate from our mind, or any part of us in fact, makes no sense from per's cultural perspective.

The views that do not separate mind and body seem to be more in line with what we now know about the way people work from interpersonal neurobiology. We are a complex system and we're connected to each other's nervous systems, and the larger ecosystem, through co-regulation.

Take a moment to consider the way you were brought up, the beliefs in your culture of origin and the culture where you live now. Maybe you were brought up bi- or even tri-cultural. If so, please take the time you need to consider all the cultural influences in your life. What have you learned about the way you work? Have you learned that body and mind are separate or one? Have you learned that the mind is more powerful than the body, or vice versa? What are the messages you received growing up and are currently receiving about bodies? Where do they come from? What do you believe about body, mind/body, or any other way in which you might view yourself? Note your current beliefs and the places where they come from below...

. . . .

. . . .

. . . .

. . . .

. . . .

. . . .

. . . .

In this book, we've often talked about a trauma-informed approach. This is definitely based on an understanding of how our nervous system works and how our body is deeply connected with our mind. In fact, our brain is in our body, it's an organ in our body and we could say it's an integral part of our body! However, neurobiology has also been revealing something that many healers already knew: we don't think just with our brain! We have different communication pathways within us and they're all connected to one another. Imagine an intricate system of highways, including roundabouts and main exchange stations! It would be beyond the scope of this book to really get into the way our nervous system works, but it's worth noting that the brain is only one of the communication pathways in our body.

Other central nervous system pathways include the spinal cord. This is surrounded by cerebrospinal fluid, which is protected by three more layers called the meninges. Through the peripheral nervous system, impulses travel along the spinal cord, to and from the brain, and bring messages to specific locations in the body. Basically, the spinal cord helps us move hands, feet, arms and legs, as well as controlling other organs in our body. This is why, when we're scared, our spine might feel as if it's going completely rigid and we can't move. At times, we might also feel mobilized to run away, or experience our head as detached from our body, or feel as if we could crumble to the floor and never move again.

However, our complex communication system doesn't stop at brain and spine. The stomach—or gut—has a part to play in this system too. You might have experienced feeling nauseous or having a stomach ache when you're nervous or overwhelmed, for example. That's because the gut is where more nervous system connections live! In fact, there are so many neuron networks there that some scientists are calling our gut a "second brain." One of the primary nerves in the gut, the vagus, carries information up to the brain, which means our emotions and our responses are also, literally, governed by our gut.

There is so much more to say on all of this, but it would take an entire book to do so! Instead, for now, take a moment to breathe and check in with your body. You may want to pay particular attention to your head, your spine and your gut. What's happening there? What are the sensations you're experiencing? For example, does your spine feel tight or relaxed? How about your jaw? Does your head feel "full" or "buzzy" or some other sensation? How about your stomach? Is it clenching or expansive or something else? Once you feel you've explored those three parts, you might want to move to your arms and hands, legs and feet. What's happening there?

As ever, feel free to adapt this exercise according to the sensations available to you. You can check in with those parts of yourself by focusing your breath there (you can even use the focusing technique from Chapter 11, if you like) or by gently moving, remembering that to breathe is to move and that micro (small) movements can be just as important and bring as much insight as macro (large) movements. Once you've had a thorough check-in with yourself, you might want to note what you've noticed below, either using words, colors, drawing or anything else that might be useful for you.

We talked earlier about emotions as information. How do we even know that we're having an emotion? Emotions start from sensations in the body. For example, when we feel fear, our back might seize up, or our feet might get restless and itchy as if they want to run away. For this exercise, you might want to go back to the feeling wheel in Chapter 9. Use the emotions at the center of the wheel (Mad, Scared, Joyful, Powerful, Peaceful, Sad) or any other basic emotions that make sense to you. Then use some colors and/or keywords to indicate how those emotions feel in your body, either by using the map on the next page (as in the exercise in Chapter 5 when we mapped trauma responses in the body) or by using a larger piece of paper to draw the outline of your own body, or in some other way that works for you.

To help you with this exercise, you can think of a time when you felt those emotions. However, please use memories where those emotions were present and manageable, rather than really traumatic memories. We don't want you to become distressed just for the sake of an exercise! If you notice starting to feel overwhelmed or numb, please stop and take time to ground and take care of yourself.

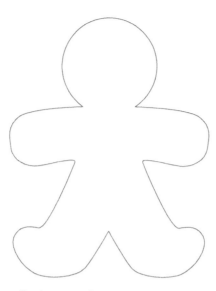

Bodymap of my core emotions

In this chapter, we've discussed mind/body and cultural views on how we work as humans, as well as introduced some ideas about our nervous system from neurobiology, and then we mapped core emotions in our body. So, what does this all have to do with self-care? We believe that it's challenging to care consensually for ourselves and others if we don't have a relationship with ourselves, including all the ways in which communication happens within us.

This is why we have spent a few pages talking about the nervous system and encouraging you to map emotions in your body/self. In order to take care of ourselves and others, we need to have a felt sense of where we are. Do we have a sense of what "yes," "no" or "maybe" feel like in our body (more in Chapter 23)? Do we know what the very early stages of sadness, anger, fear, peace, confidence or joy feel like in our body/self?

Let's take a moment to revisit the map from the previous exercise and the one from Chapter 5 and connect some dots now. Take a moment to map, in whatever way makes sense to you, your core emotions, the sensations that let you know those core emotions are happening, and overlay also your trauma/ survival responses (fight, flight, freeze, fawn—the four Fs). We hope this will start to give you a more complete picture of how we're always in communication with ourselves, if we take the time to listen. When we know how emotions and survival responses feel in our body, we can start to recognize them sooner and take care of ourselves in ways that allow us to be more present to our own needs and, when appropriate, the needs of others.

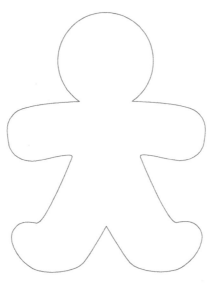

Bodymap of my core emotions, sensations and four Fs

You might have guessed by now that we truly believe that our bodies (i.e. ourselves, if we feel there is no mind/body separation) are the guide! So, right now, take a moment to get in touch with your body and notice: What do you need right here, right now? Can you meet that need? If not, is there a need that you can meet right now that would make you feel even 5 percent more comfortable? This can be as simple as changing your posture, getting a cushion for added support, or taking a breath, or two. Go on, listen to yourself and see what you can offer your hard-working self in this moment.

"What you seek is seeking you." (Rumi)

What if much of the wisdom and care you're looking for was already there, in your body, waiting for you to listen?

CHAPTER 14

Your Relationship With Your Body

Doesn't that all sound so simple? We're well aware it's not simple at all. In fact, the following chapter (15) is all about feeling that having/being a body might be intolerable. As survivors of a range of traumas, we know that having a relationship with our body/self can be complicated.

For example, we might have received really oppressive messages about our body/self, and our needs, from the culture around us, our families, our peers and so on. So in this chapter, we'll take some time to reflect on where messages about our embodied selves come from, whether they have changed from the past to the present, and whether we have desired messages we want to call in to ourselves.

You may remember the diagram on the next page from previous exercises. In Chapter 10 we used it to explore your relationship with feelings. Now, we'll use it again to explore the relationship with your body. For this exercise, we'd like to invite you to think about all these different levels in the past and the present, and then to map desired messages you'd like to learn/deepen about your body/self.

Let's start with messages about your body that you might have from the past. Think and note the messages in each layer: the world and wider culture, community and institutions, close relationships, and within you.

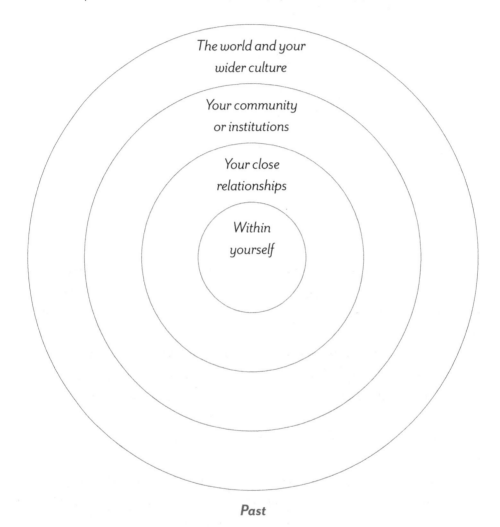

The world and your
wider culture

Your community
or institutions

Your close
relationships

Within
yourself

Past

Now that you've looked at the past, including intergenerational and historical messages you received about your body/self, let's look at your current relationship.

Think about the messages in each layer: the world and wider culture, community and institutions, close relationships and within you. What current messages do you receive about your body/embodied self in each layer right now? You might like to write, draw, or paste in illustrations of these messages on the diagram below.

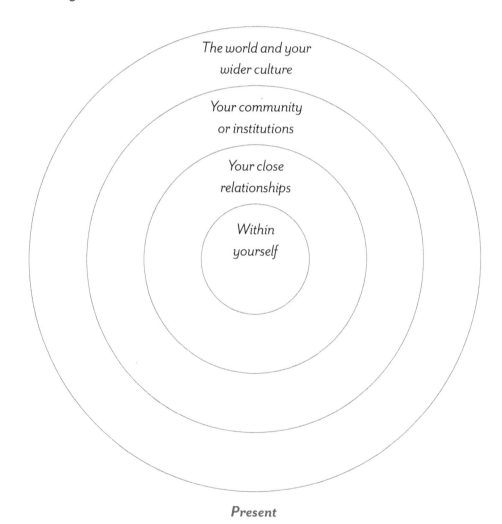

Present

Now that we've considered the past and the present, let's think about desired, intentional messages about your body/self that you'd like to invite, nurture, cultivate and deepen relationship with. Think about these messages in each layer: the world and wider culture, community and institutions, close relationships and within you. What are your desired messages for each layer right now? This is your wish, not just for yourself but also for your close relationships, communities, wider culture and the world. Another way to think about this might be: What is the spell you desire to manifest when it comes to messages about embodiment? You might like to write, draw, or paste in illustrations of these messages on the diagram below.

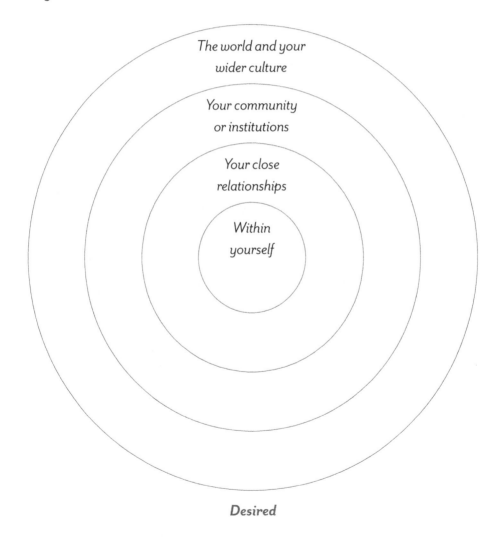

The world and your
wider culture

Your community
or institutions

Your close
relationships

Within
yourself

Desired

You may remember that we talked about altars as a practice in Chapter 8. If you have an altar, you might even want to place the "desired" diagram on it, once finished. This can then be a focus for the messages you want to cultivate about your body/self within yourself, your close relationships, the communities and institutions you might be part of, your wider culture and the world.

As you've explored the messages you've received in the past—and are still receiving in the present—you may have noticed some obstacles to being able to have a loving relationship with your body/self. Let us be clear: we're not among those who believe you have to love yourself first before others can love you. We feel that message tends to individualize much more systemic issues and obstacles to loving ourselves! What we're talking about here is recognizing that there might be systemic issues that get in the way of a kind and loving relationship with our body/self.

For example, many of us live under ongoing settler-colonial regimes, and cultures in which we're getting hateful and oppressive messages about our bodies/selves if we don't fit into a very narrow, normative narrative. Those hateful and oppressive messages are like the air we breathe—they're all around us and it can be very challenging to ignore them. Even if we do ignore them, it doesn't mean they have not snuck in somehow, given that they're so pervasive and insidious! It's incredibly challenging, if not impossible, to completely step outside dominant culture.

If we're trans, queer, black, brown, Indigenous, immigrant, fat, disabled, femme, old, a sex worker or have any other identities or experiences that are stigmatized, stereotyped and oppressed within dominant culture, it can be incredibly challenging to overcome those messages. It can be helpful, at those times, to remember that we're not alone and that those obstacles are systemic and not just individual.

Let's take some time now to reflect on what systemic obstacles we might be facing when it comes to having a kind and loving relationship with our body/self. We've provided you below with some examples of systemic oppression, but please feel free to add your own and expand this list. Note which kind of systemic oppression you face, and write down, draw or reflect on which negative messages about your body/self go along with this type of oppression and might be an obstacle for you. For example, we might write down "transphobia" and then note messages like "nobody is going to love your trans body" by its side or connect it to transphobia with an arrow.

Racism	Fatphobia	Cisgenderism
Colorism	Misogyny	Ageism
Xenophobia	Toxic masculinity	Whorephobia
Ableism	Transphobia	

. . . .

. . . .

. . . .

. . . .

This exercise about systemic obstacles might have got you down. After all, those obstacles can seem so much vaster than us. How could we possibly counter oppression so vast? We discussed in Chapter 2 how foundational Audre Lorde's definition of self-care as a political act is to the way we approach self-care. We acknowledge that she was talking within the context of being a queer, black woman in the US, and we strive not to whitewash her words for our own purposes. Black women and Indigenous scholars and activists are indeed at the forefront of ways of thinking about care for self and others because their survival has been/is indeed dependent on finding anti-colonial pathways to liberation.

We want to be accomplices to those struggles and each other's struggles. If, ultimately, we're aiming for liberation, and we sure hope we are, then we need to treat ourselves and one another in liberatory ways, as Audre Lorde and other black, Indigenous and disabled scholars, authors and activists continue to remind us. This means treating ourselves, and others, in ways that are consensual, intentional, relational and counter to violent, colonial, oppressive messages. This has to include our relationship with our body/self.

As Sonya Renee Taylor, author of *The Body is Not an Apology: The Power of Radical Self-Love*, writes in a longer poem published on the blog *The Body is Not an Apology* on August 26, 2013:

The body is not calamity. The body is not a math test. The body is not a wrong answer. The body is not a failed class. You are not failing. The body is not an apology. The body is not a crime, is not a gun. The body is not crime, is not sentence to be served. It is not prison, is not pavement, is not prayer. The body is not an apology.

This might seem a good time to remind you that if you're struggling to love your body/self, it's OK, it's understandable, it's more than reasonable in this oppressive world. Please remember that this book is not a stick with which to beat yourself up even more; self-care cannot become another oppressive tool with which to police ourselves. All we're inviting you to do is to enter into a kind and loving relationship with your body/self or, if you're already in one, celebrate it. As Alex's beloved Donald Engstrom-Reese would say: Are you willing to be willing?

If you're willing to enter into a loving relationship with your body/self, or if you already are in one, we'd like to invite you to take a moment, and the space below, to write a poem, draw, create a symbol, use some colors, or dance, to show this willingness to nurture this relationship as much as you're able right now and as gently as you can...

CHAPTER 15

We Are Embodied, But What if It's Intolerable?

We've talked about the importance of the body and explored your relationship with your body/self. However, what if you don't experience yourself as an embodied self? This might happen for a range of reasons, including trauma, depersonalization, neurodivergence, chronic pain or fatigue, or dissociative responses. That's OK. Feeling disconnected from our embodied self is a very human experience! It's an experience that many of us have at some point or another. That feeling of "zoning out" and not even knowing how you got somewhere when walking, biking or driving is a form of internal disconnect that most of us are familiar with.

There is nothing wrong with not experiencing yourself as an embodied being. We believe we can still take care of ourselves when we don't feel very embodied. How can we do this? Routines are one way in which we can take care of ourselves, even when we don't feel connected to our body/self, or have trouble connecting. Daily routines remind us that we need food, water and sleep to function. Weekly routines remind us that we need time to rest, unplug and connect with other humans and/or nature. We can choose which routines are most supportive for us (see Chapter 5).

If you feel disembodied but would like a better relationship with your body, another way to go about it is to be gentle with yourself and to increase very, very slowly the amount of connection you have with your body/self. Why go slowly? Because the body is slower than our prefrontal cortex, which often wants us to rush through things. We don't want to overwhelm our nervous system with too much information at once! You might want to pick some of the practices about presence from Chapter 11 and remember the cradle of kindness from Chapter 4, and try out some activities slowly, over time.

Another way you might want to start exploring your embodied self is externally rather than internally. What do we mean by this? Well, for example, you might want to spend time coloring and noticing which colors feel more or less pleasing; or crafting and noticing which textures, images and sensations seem more or less pleasing to you. You can also notice your interaction with external elements. How does air feel on different days? What about the warmth of the sun in different seasons? What about water? Is there a body of water you like to be with? Why is that? Notice your experiences with the environment around you and, if you like, make some notes on your responses to these questions here.

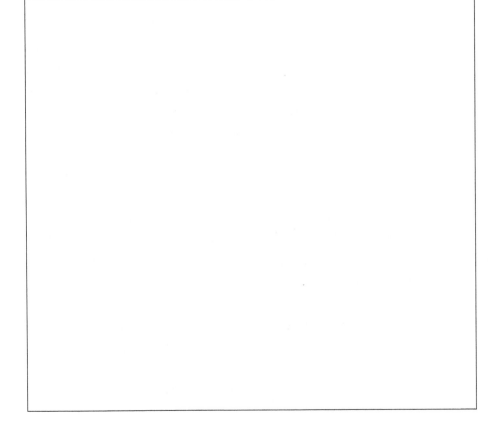

Once more, go slow with all of this and feel free to note below what—besides systemic obstacles explored earlier—might be an internal barrier to the relationship between you and your body/self. Feel free to experiment if you're curious about embodiment and to let it be, if you're not and you are content to carry on as you were.

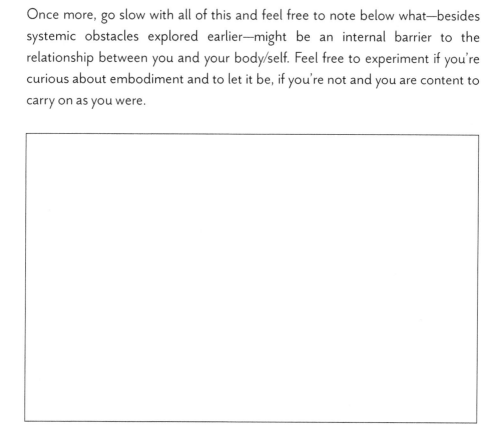

Another issue that might be in the way of us developing a relationship with our body/self is if we feel somehow betrayed by our body. We mentioned ableism earlier, which is definitely a systemic barrier for those of us who are disabled. The social model of disability encapsulates the idea that being disabled is not inherent to a person, but rather that we're systemically disabled by the way in which dominant culture organizes things. For example, it's not being in a wheelchair that's the issue but the fact that the world is by and large designed for non-wheelchair users that is the problem.

The social model of disability has been key in the disability justice movement. However, disabled feminist authors and activists have also criticized it for not taking into enough account the role and experience of the body. For example, if my disability means that I'm in varying degrees of pain, the social model of disability does not account for how I might feel about my body, but only for how others react to it. Also, both in the traditional model of medical disability and the social model of disability, being disabled is viewed as "other" than the norm in some way.

Disabled feminist authors challenge us to think about embodiment and systemic barriers at the same time. Within a feminist model of disability, we can feel betrayed by our body and by society at the same time. For example, we might feel that our bodies are "failing" by not being reliable, which means we might have to cancel a lot on people we know. We might also feel, at the same time, that society is failing us by expecting us to treat our bodies as machines and commodities that are impervious to fluctuations, changes in energy, focus and pain levels and so on.

This both/and view seems more expansive and allows for contradictions, such as being angry with the world for making it near to impossible, generally, to survive and thrive as a disabled person in a capitalist society, and being frustrated with our bodies for being unreliable. We might also feel betrayed when we live with chronic illness—or frequent acute illnesses—and our bodies react differently to the same things, or shift all of a sudden, or generally tend to do what they want, without our prefrontal cortex having much of a say in it!

Of course, this is not just about being disabled, but also about being human. After all, we're all only temporarily abled, until age or illness catches up with us and reminds us that our rational, prefrontal cortex cannot overrule our body/self. Take a moment to breathe that in, if this is not a concept that you've come across before. If it is, take a moment to notice how it's landing for you in this moment. How do you feel about disability? Whether you're disabled or not, take a few moments to note below your thoughts, feelings and stories about disability and what being disabled means.

We've said before that many of us live in dominant cultures that promote going fast, rather than slow, and getting as much as possible done. Does the culture you live in glorify being busy and working? If so, is that congruent with the values you received growing up? Do you find yourself saying things like "I can't be sick"? We've been there! When we find ourselves saying things like "I couldn't possibly get sick right now" or "Getting sick is not an option," it's a sure sign that we need to slow down and check in with ourselves. We've obviously let dominant culture dictate the pace again and we're spouting nonsense to ourselves. After all, getting sick is not something that is under our control!

In fact, one of the main challenges that disability poses in an ableist world is the reminder that our bodies are not entirely in our control and that we're mortal beings who can get sick and who will eventually die. We believe that the sooner we come to terms with this, the more heartache (and second arrows—see Chapter 11) we'll spare ourselves.

So many messages in dominant culture are about policing bodies to be under our control—controlling body odor, size, health and so on. This can often give us an illusion of control where we might be better served by accepting how things are—something that we'll turn to next. First, though, let's take some time to consider your relationship to sickness and getting sick.

Take a moment to note below, through story, drawing or any other way that makes sense to you, how you feel about getting sick and being sick. For example, do you recognize it immediately or do you go down kicking and screaming? Do you take time off or push through? Do you feel personally responsible for your sickness and find ways to berate yourself? Whatever and however you feel, try to be as honest as you can, whether you're someone who gets sick a lot, a little and anything in between, and whether you're disabled or not.

In her foreword to another favorite of ours, Toni Bernhard's *How to Be Sick: A Buddhist-Inspired Guide for the Chronically Ill and Their Caregivers*, Sylvia Boorstein writes, "It is a fundamental human truth, transcending cultures and traditions, that the wisest response to situations that are beyond our control, circumstances that we cannot change, is noncontention" (2018, p.xvi).

We'd like to invite you to be with your body, right here, right now, as you are. If you need ideas for practices or support, you may want to revisit Chapter 12 on finding presence, or Chapter 11, where we talked about how to stay with your feelings. We know we keep coming back to presence and that this can seem repetitive. However, we do truly believe that we need to learn to be with all of ourselves if we're to be able to care for ourselves and one another in healthy, liberatory ways. So, this is a moment for you to just be present with your body/self as it is. When we do this, we practice self-acceptance, which helps us move towards the non-contention attitude (not struggling and striving) mentioned by Toni, no matter what's happening.

Breathe, notice wherever you're at, and just be. If being present with your body is not an option right now, for whatever reason, that's OK. Let that be what it is.

Wherever you are on your journey, it's OK. Can you meet your body/self there and be at peace with what is?

Just Be

If we're struggling to be present and accept our body/self, we might also struggle with being present with and accepting of other bodies. After all, bodies can be a lot! We make noises, such as sniffles, farting, burping, talking and so on. Some of those noises are voluntary and some are involuntary. The chances are that if we're having trouble with being embodied, we might also have a hard time with people around us being embodied too.

Are there practices that can help us cultivate being present with other bodies, no matter where they're at? Compassion practices can definitely help us with this. After all, if we can tap into our common humanity, we can soften around other bodies/selves, and, it is hoped, ours too. So, how can we be compassionate with other bodies/selves?

There are many practices for compassion out there, and an internet search will quickly point you in a range of directions. However, no matter the technique, compassion means, at the heart, to feel, suffer and be human together.

Next time you find yourself being near other bodies, take time to notice your reactions. Do you want to fight them, do you want to get away, do you want to please them, or do you feel uncertain of what to do, frozen on the spot? If so, you may be having one of the four Fs. Be gently curious about where those feelings are coming from and try to breathe through them. If they become near intolerable, please stop and do something else.

Keep doing this when you're around other bodies/selves. Are there things that you find particularly challenging, uncomfortable or unpleasant? For example, farting or belching? Are these things that you try to keep under tight control for yourself? If you find yourself judging others for their bodies, is it because you were judged or learned somewhere that certain aspects of ourselves should be judged harshly? You may want to revisit the activity in Chapter 14 to help you make sense of the messages you received about bodies.

Try to keep noticing with gentle curiosity how your sensations, emotions and physical reactions rise and fall. As much as possible, try to hold them all with open hands so you can pick them up and put them down. For example, you might notice, "There's a racist thought" or, "There goes a fatphobic feeling." When we can stay present with those reactions, with open hands, we can slowly learn how to be with other bodies/selves with less fear of reactions from our own body/self. Take it slow and only do as much as you can, as often as you're able. Remember, there is no rush. These are practices for a lifetime.

If you want, take note through writing, drawing or whatever makes sense to you of what you're learning when you're present with other bodies/selves.

CHAPTER 16

Working With Your Body
in Self-Caring Ways

However you feel about your body/self, as we said before, there are ways in which you can take care of yourself. We mentioned routines as being helpful. Sometimes having something similar to a car manual can also be helpful! For example, if we're having a hard time taking care of ourselves, or if we're grieving, or sick, a manual or user's guide can be a great way to remember and communicate what we need.

We'd like to encourage you to create such a manual or user's guide right now. You can even give it a cover and a title. For example, *Alex's User's Guide to Alex*. Not very original, but it does the job! So grab some paper, pencils or pens, and let's get going if you like.

Things you might want to think about are: What are the daily practices needed, such as eating, sleeping a certain number of hours and so on? What are the routines that help you meet those daily needs? What are the weekly needs? What about yearly needs? You may want to go back to the activity towards the end of Chapter 5 and build from there. You don't need to reinvent the wheel, just write down all the things that help you take care of your embodied self on a regular, semi-regular and even irregular basis, such as WRAP plans in times of crisis. You might like to make some notes here about what you'd like to include in the manual, and maybe go away later to create the manual itself in the form of a zine or set of cards, for example.

Having this type of document can be really handy when we're in crisis or struggling, or if we need others to take care of us. It'll save a lot of our energy in those moments when we need it most! If this is not a good time for you to create something like this, that's OK too. Just know that this is an option and, for now, let it go. It's OK if this is not for you. It's always OK to be wherever you're at.

As well as meeting some of your basic bodily needs, you might have started to think about somatic reflective self-care practices. We briefly mentioned those in Chapter 7. We want to spend a little more time here with embodied—also known as somatic—reflective self-care practices.

For example, in Chapter 7 we briefly mentioned authentic movement. Somatic self-care reflective practices help us deepen the connection with our own body/self, beyond everyday maintenance. Given that we believe that emotions live in the body, creating times when we can purposefully and intentionally be with ourselves in reflective ways can be really important.

We've already mentioned practices such as focusing, wandering and wondering and so on. What we'd like you to do now, if you're up for it, is to pick one of those practices, try it out and then come back and note in the space on the next page what your experience was like. Was this a familiar or unfamiliar practice? Were you comfortable or uncomfortable engaging in this? Did you learn something new or did it reinforce things you already knew? Were you bored? Would you try it out again or not really? Basically, just take time to notice and note how the somatic reflective self-care practice was for you.

If you need some inspiration and you don't want to go back through the book, here's a simple movement reflective self-care practice.

- Choose an intention. For example, I want to explore my relationship with my hands. Or, I am open to knowing what expansion feels like in my body/self.

- Decide if you want music or not. If you choose to have music, you might even create a playlist to match your intention and the desired length of practice. For example, you might want to choose music that makes you feel expansive, and practice for 15 minutes, so you choose 15 minutes of music to combine in one playlist.

- Whether you use music or not, start from a place of comfort. This could be sitting, lying down or anywhere else. Listen to your body/self as you open to your intention.

- Wait to move until you feel your body is moving you, rather than being guided by your prefrontal cortex (conscious thoughts and choices). Don't overthink it. It doesn't need to be perfect; just do the best you can.

- Experiment, play and move with your intention. Be gentle, curious and try to refrain from self-judgment.

- Once the movement practice is over, take some time to debrief by yourself through writing, drawing, a voice memo, or by talking with a trusted person.

. . . .

. . . .

. . . .

. . . .

What would it look like to partner with your body/self? Maybe you've already done so, maybe you haven't, or you have thought about it but decided it wasn't the right time. When we commit to other people, we often write down what we're committing to. For example, if we commit to writing a book, we might write a contract. If we commit to a child as a supporting adult in their lives, we might make promises in front of a community. If we commit to a country, we might pledge allegiance to that country or that country's leaders. If we commit to a religion or spiritual path, we might make pledges in front of deities, ancestors or community.

If you were to commit to your body/self, what kind of contract, vows, pledges or promises might you make? Pick something that feels comfortable for you and your culture. Once you have picked something, note in the space on the next page what your contract, vows, promises or pledges are. You can also choose symbols, drawings, colors or movements to represent those.

We've talked a lot about somatic maintenance, connection and even commitment, but what about joy and pleasure? After all, one of the advantages of being embodied is having the capacity to experience joy and pleasure. We can experience the sun touching our skin, water flowing over us, the caress of a lover, our own self-touch, a pleasing smell, a delicious taste. To be embodied is to feel.

We often think of the erotic as being connected to sex and sexuality, but the erotic is our capacity to feel alive, connected and vibrant. As Audre Lorde once more teaches us, in her essay "Uses of the Erotic: The Erotic as Power":

> This is one reason why the erotic is so feared, and so often relegated to the bedroom alone, when it is recognized at all. For once we begin to feel deeply all the aspects of our lives, we begin to demand from ourselves and from our life-pursuits that they feel in accordance with that joy which we know ourselves to be capable of. (2012, p.57)

What is the joy that you know yourself to be capable of? What nourishes you, helps you feel rejuvenated, refreshed and alive? What makes your body shiver with delight and anticipation? What are your embodied pleasures? Your favorite food, smells, touch (including self-touch, of course), dances, rhythms and more? Take some time to note them in the space on the next page through words, drawings, symbols and whatever else makes sense to you. Create your own pleasure map.

We've asked you to create your own pleasure map and to consider the erotic beyond, as well as within—if you want—the sexual realm, but why? We believe, alongside many other people, that to move forward in our own care and the care of others, we need to be in touch with pleasure in our lives. In the dominant Anglo cultures we live in, motivation to care for self and others seems to come from a sense of duty and obligation. But what if caring for ourselves and one another—and our own activism—come from pleasure?

adrienne maree brown writes in *Pleasure Activism: The Politics of Feeling Good*: "Pleasure activism is the work we do to reclaim our whole, happy, and satisfiable selves from the impacts, delusions, and limitations of oppression and/ or supremacy" (2019, p.13).

If caring for yourself puts pleasure as the foundation and the lead, what would self-care look like? If pleasure itself was a valuable endpoint, what would your care for yourself and others look like in your life right now? Take the time to imagine and re-imagine all the work done so far. Is pleasure there? If not, how would adding pleasure change things? What would caring for your body/self, being with your body/self and being with other bodies/selves look like if pleasure was the guide?

Take your time to dream, imagine, re-imagine, invent, explore and make up care through the lens of pleasure...

M.Y.O. Slow Down Page

What's your slow pleasure right now?

Selves Care

(Your Plural Selves)

CHAPTER 17

Yourself as Plural and a Work in Progress

At the start of this book, we spoke about how the ways we're encouraged to treat ourselves in dominant culture are often the opposite of self-care. Criticism culture encourages us to constantly monitor ourselves; comparing ourselves against others or ideals, and finding ourselves wanting; improving and perfecting ourselves, or—if we can't—giving up on and neglecting ourselves.

We've talked about how this way of doing things is deeply rooted in neoliberal Anglo consumer capitalism. This is invested in convincing individuals that they are not good enough, so they buy more products. It also encourages people to individualize, to look within themselves to fix things, rather than looking outwards to address social injustice and change the structures and systems around them, which are often the major cause of their suffering.

For all these reasons—as you've probably found by now—self-care can be incredibly challenging. How can we care for this self that we've spent a lifetime policing, criticizing, and trying to "fix"? How can we nourish ourselves when we're so used to individualizing our suffering, and blaming and shaming ourselves for it?

One answer to this is to start from a radically different understanding of the self. Dominant culture sees the self as *singular* and *fixed*. This assumption has been questioned in two important ways which point us towards an alternative, kinder, way of relating to ourselves and others. This is the idea that we're:

- *plural* rather than singular

- in process—or *fluid*—rather than static.

The idea that you are a singular self, which remains pretty much the same over time, may well seem so obvious that questioning it is a strange thing to do, but that's exactly what we're going to do in this chapter.

We'll unpack what these ideas mean more over the next few pages, and then spend Chapters 18 and 19 on plural selves, and Chapter 20 on the self in process.

For now, just take a moment for these ideas to sink in. Do they resonate with you at all at this point? In what ways might you experience yourself as plural? In what ways as fluid—or changing over time? How might these ways of experiencing yourself relate to being kind—or caring—for yourself?

. . . .

. . . .

. . . .

. . . .

. . . .

. . . .

. . . .

. . . .

. . . .

. . . .

Beginning with the idea of being plural, rather than singular, various therapeutic, spiritual and philosophical models have come to the understanding that some, or all, people experience themselves as more than one self some, or all, of the time. Here are just a few of them. You can read more about these ideas in the resources at the end of the book if you're interested.

- Various therapeutic models which suggest we all have parent, adult and child states (or similar) within us (e.g. gestalt therapy, transactional analysis, or internal family systems theory).

- Various Indigenous understandings of people as having the capacity to embody multiple ancestors and/or deities.

- The Plural Pride Movement which reclaims mental health diagnoses of dissociative identity disorder (previously multiple personality disorder) and understands people who are diagnosed in this way as systems.

- Philosophical ideas that there is a collective unconscious of archetypes which we can all draw on in shaping ourselves.

- Latina feminist approaches which see the self as multiple, including the work of Gloria Anzaldúa and Mariana Ortega.

- Therapeutic models of subpersonalities which suggest that it's helpful for most of us to get in touch with different sides of ourselves—such as our inner child or our inner critic.

- Spiritual beliefs that we carry past lives within us.

- Creative understandings which see the characters we create in fiction and fantasy as aspects of ourselves, or where creators create under different personas.

- Trauma-informed understandings which see ourselves as becoming stuck at different ages and/or relating between multiple past versions of ourselves.

The author Walt Whitman famously said, "Do I contradict myself? Very well then, I contradict myself. I am large, I contain multitudes."

Before we go on to an activity, think for yourself whether any of these approaches are familiar to you, or whether you know of any other ways of understanding the self as plural, or multiple. Do these ideas—or this quote—resonate with you at all? Make some notes in response to this question, below, if you like.

One way that helps many people make sense of this idea of plurality—for themselves—is to think about how they are in different relationships and/or different situations. Let's try it.

Write the names of five important people in your life in the boxes along the top of the grid below—for example, a family member, an old friend, a good colleague, an online mate, someone you live with. It's OK if you do it with fewer than five people, or choose companion animals, fictional characters you relate to or any other relationships which make sense to you. Under each person put an "X" if you mostly behave in the way described on the left of the grid with that person. Put a "0" if you mostly behave in the way described on the right of the grid. Leave it blank if neither fits.

So, in the example row we've completed, we'd be outgoing with person 1 and person 2, shy with person 3 and person 5, and neither term really applies to how we are with person 4.

X	Person 1:	Person 2:	Person 3:	Person 4:	Person 5:	0
	_____	_____	_____	_____	_____	
Outgoing	X	X	0		0	Shy
Fun						Serious
Protective of them						Protected by them
They take control						I take control
Patient						Impatient
Emotional						Unemotional
Responsible						Free
I can really be myself						I can't really be myself

Reflect on the patterns of Xs and Os. Are you the same self in different relationships?

The psychologist whom we both knew and loved, Trevor Butt, used this grid in his research. He got people to create their own opposites on the left- and right-hand sides, based on what was meaningful to them. For some people for example, the opposite of "serious" would be "fun"; for others it might be "silly," "playful," "childlike," or "immature." For some people, the opposite of "emotional" would be "rational," "calm," or "cold," rather than "unemotional." For some, seriousness and emotionality wouldn't be such important issues in their perceptions of themselves, but something else might be, such as how nurturing they got to be in that relationship, how honest they felt or how chatty they were. If you found the activity straightforward, you might like to have another go, but creating your own table with opposites on the left and right that are more meaningful to you.

Trevor was particularly interested in comparing how people experienced themselves in relationships where they felt they could "really be themselves": the ones where they put an X in the last row. Everyone agreed it was important to have relationships where they could be themselves. However, what this meant varied remarkably from relationship to relationship. People could feel they were being themselves in relationships where they acted in seemingly completely opposite ways. For example, they might be playful and extroverted with one friend, and serious and introverted with another. They might be patient, deferential and protected with a parent, and impatient, dominant and protective with a partner.

You could do a similar activity for different situations, rather than different relationships. You could reflect on who you are in a work meeting, in bed at night, going to a party, walking with a friend, or in the midst of a crisis, for example.

Whichever version of the activity we do, for many people it reveals that our selves are more complex than we initially thought. Although all of the selves feel equally "true"—we feel "ourselves" when we're being them—somewhat different characters seem to be drawn out of us by different relationships or situations. Think about times when you've got together with family or old school friends and suddenly a part of yourself emerged that you'd almost forgotten about: perhaps the teasing older sibling or the gawky teenager. Similarly, we can feel stuck when others only see a certain aspect of us, and we find ourselves playing along with this—for example, if an auto-recovery person treats you as a damsel in distress, or if you bump into a business client out at the pub and find yourself acting all professional in that social context. Are these kinds of examples familiar to you?

People vary a lot in terms of how they experience plurality. There's no "right" way to experience it, and it may not even resonate with you at all (in which case, feel free to skip Chapters 18 and 19). For example, people find their experience in different places on the following spectrums. You might reflect for yourself where you are on these, if indeed they resonate at all:

- How coherent/unified to diverse/plural we experience ourselves as being.

- How many selves we experience from none to one to several to hundreds.

- How muted to vivid our experience of our different selves alters, or our subpersonalities is.

- How separate to overlapping these different parts are.

- How much we do, or don't, experience dissociation or forgetting between the times when different parts of us are to the fore, or fronting.

- To what extent our plurality is rooted in traumatic experience, and/or the extent of the trauma that we've experienced.

How do we get to the point of being plural selves? We're back to our old friend, this diagram:

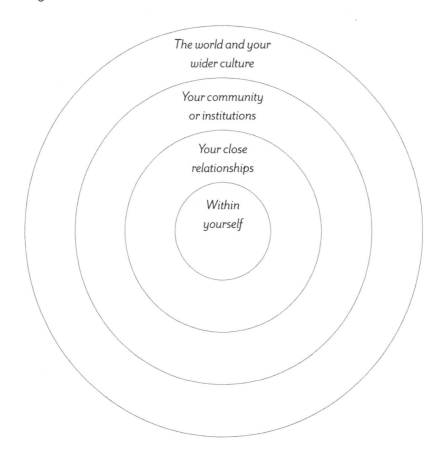

As we grow up, we learn which sides of us are welcomed by others, and which are not; which get us what we want, and which don't. This is shaped by these interrelated forces: wider culture; communities and institutions; families, peers and other close relationships; and how we relate within our internal landscape. You might want to use the diagram here to reflect on which characteristics were encouraged in you—on each of these levels—and which were discouraged.

We'll say more about the model of foregrounding—and disowning—different selves in Chapter 18, and then more about how to balance this out and get ourselves working as a team in Chapter 19. The two main aims of plural selves work are to:

· identify and embrace all our selves

· improve communication between the selves so that they can work together.

For now, how does this relate to self-care and being kinder towards ourselves? Our sense is that it can often be easier to treat ourselves kindly if we understand ourselves as plural in some way. For example, MJ finds it hard to treat themself kindly as a whole, but finds it relatively easy for their older selves to treat their younger selves kindly, or for part of themself who is feeling vulnerable to get support from part of themself that is feeling stronger on a particular day.

As well as being plural, many thinkers suggest that we're a work in progress, rather than being a fixed self which stays relatively stable over time.

Think about this for a moment. Put some ages in this table and reflect on the ways in which you feel like the same person—and a different person—to who you were back then.

Point in life	Age I was	Ways I felt like the same person I am now	Ways I felt like a different person to the one/s I am now
Baby			
Child			
Teenager			
One-third my age now			
Half my age now			
Two-thirds my age now			

We'll unpack this idea of being fluid, a work in process, or becoming something over time, more in Chapter 20. It relates to plurality because we can also then relate with the different versions of ourselves that we were in the past or that we might become in the future.

How does this idea relate to self-care and being kind to ourselves? A nice metaphor for being in process comes from Buddhist author Stephen Batchelor. He suggests we're like the pot spinning on the wheel, and the potter who spins it, drawing it up higher, pressing it lower, always in motion and evolving. When we see ourselves as static, it's like putting the pot in a kiln and fixing it. When we fix ourselves, we become rigid, brittle and fragile. Of course, we may want to fix ourselves, because we hope that we might be able to remain forever as the person we most like being at the best of times. Also, being fixed feels much more certain and controllable: this is who I am and this is how I do things. And if we can present a fixed, good, self to the rest of the world, we hope they won't see how we're flawed. However, because we're not really fixed, our fluid life moves on. The self we're trying to cling to may not fit it any more, or another aspect of ourselves breaks through and shatters the carefully fixed object.

Fixity can also be dangerous because we might end up feeling fixed as the aspects of ourselves that we're least comfortable with, or see as most flawed. If we recognize our fluidity, then those things may not be so threatening, because we know they're only one part of us. They'll inevitably shift and change over time because we're always becoming something different. It's only when we fix ourselves that we feel frozen and stuck in someone we really don't want to be—that unbearable feeling that this is all we've ever been and all we'll ever be. It's not about changing for change's sake, but rather being open to change and aware of ourselves as a process.

CHAPTER 18

Identifying Your Plural Selves

Over the next two chapters we're going to give you lots of ideas for how to *identify* your plural selves, and how to work with them, which involves putting them into *communication* with each other and helping them to work as a team. Again, if the experience of plurality doesn't resonate with you at all, it's fine to skip these chapters and go on to Chapter 20.

Chapters 18 and 19 between them cover the two main aims of plural selves work. Remember, these are:

- identifying and embracing all our selves

- improving communication between the selves so that they can work together.

As we've said, the idea is that, as we grow up, we learn that parts of ourselves are welcomed, and parts are not, in the world around us. Trauma experiences in particular can lead us to foreground parts of ourselves and disown—or cast out—others in order to survive. A useful way of visualizing this is the iceberg.

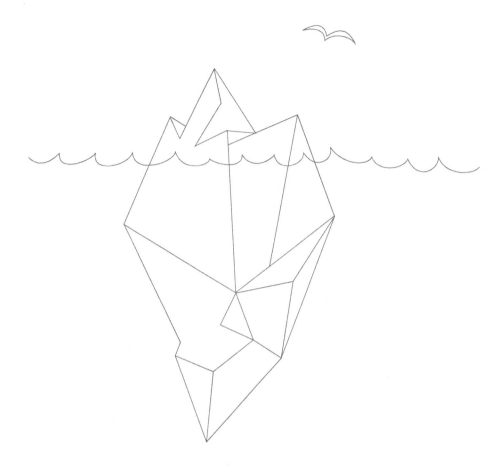

You can draw or write on this diagram the aspects of yourself which were encouraged—or foregrounded—above the surface of the water, and the aspects which were discouraged—or disowned: pushed down below the surface.

For example, one person's iceberg might have "happy," "pleasing," "cheerful" and "nice" above the surface, and "outspoken," "firm," "judgmental" and "grumpy" under the surface. For another person, those might be reversed because the latter characteristics were how they learned to survive the world, and the former ones weren't acceptable for a person like them in the time and place they were growing up.

Because of the different messages we each receive from our cultures, communities and close relationships, each person develops different selves and finds that different ones get foregrounded and disowned. However, there are some common cultural patterns to this. Many of us develop controlling sides based on fitting into the wider culture we find ourselves in, and disown the sides which are unwelcome in that culture (e.g. characteristics associated with "the opposite gender," "unacceptable" aspects of our sexuality or "negative emotions"—see Chapter 9), as well as sides which are more vulnerable.

A common model in dominant culture is for people to foreground selves which help them to control and please themselves—and others—and to disown selves which are regarded as too vulnerable or otherwise socially unacceptable. This relates to self-monitoring and self-policing which we've mentioned a few times over the course of this workbook. Here, we'll say something about how we relate to the foregrounded selves, and on the next pages how we relate to the disowned ones.

One of the selves which is perhaps most familiar to us all is the "inner critic," so we'll focus on that here, but all these ideas also apply to other foregrounded selves. Whole books have been devoted to the inner critic because it can become so harsh, toxic and destructive. We can see it as the internalizing of the criticism culture in which many of us are embedded.

To give you a sense of the inner critic, here are some of the things our inner critics had to say to us as we were working on this book: "It's not as good as your last one..." "You're losing your touch..." "...if you ever had it." "You can't say that..." "You're going to get something wrong and people will hate you..." "...maybe they already do." "It's too much..." "It's not enough..."

Given the harshness of the inner critic and the cruel, contradictory nature of the things it has to say, you might think that the thing to do with it would be to shut it up, fight it and, ideally, get rid of it. So you might be very surprised to hear that all of the advice in the literature is actually to do the opposite: to listen to it, to embrace it and to help it become an ally.

The idea here is that the inner critic and other foregrounded selves generally come from a place of trying to protect us and to help us survive. Because they are so harsh, we often stop listening to them or try to battle them. This often means that they become louder and more scary over time because they are desperate to be heard. If we can find out how to listen to them, without giving them all the power, then they can become helpful allies rather than loud, frightening enemies.

If you feel able to, you might like to have a go at drawing or collaging your own inner critic in the space on the next page and/or writing a list of some of the things it frequently has to say to you, to start to get to know it a little better. In Chapter 19, you'll learn more about how you might communicate with it. If this feels too scary, though, please feel free to leave this activity and come back to it. Facing the inner critic can be painful indeed, and it took us many years before we felt able to do it (and it's still a work in progress). If yours is a tough one, then it's fine to get support to do this work or wait until it feels doable for you. The emotional thermometer from Chapter 11 might help you to judge when it feels a good time for you to do an activity like this.

My inner critic

Our disowned selves are often the ones which are less known to us, because they are the sides of us that we've pushed down or cast out over the years. We may visualize them as sides of ourselves that we've kept locked in the basement or tried to eradicate entirely.

One of the disowned selves which is perhaps most familiar to us all is the "inner child," so we'll focus on that here, but all the ideas on this page also apply to other disowned selves.

If the idea with foregrounded selves is to listen to them carefully but give them less power, or even allow them to rest and retreat a bit, then the idea with disowned selves is often to bring them forward more, getting to know them better and helping them to develop and grow.

We often disown the child parts of ourselves because culturally we're told to leave childish things behind as we grow up, or that it isn't OK to be vulnerable or needy. Many of us—through trauma—had to become adults too quickly, and even to parent the other people around us while we were still children.

Child parts of ourselves—and there may be more than one—can hold a lot of pain and trauma. They can be the vulnerable and sensitive parts of us. They can be free and wild, the people we were before we learned what was "acceptable" or "appropriate." They can be imaginative, believing in magic and fantasy worlds.

If you feel able to, you might like to have a go at drawing or collaging your own inner child—or children—here, to start to get to know them a little better. In Chapter 19, you'll learn more about how you might communicate with them. If this feels too difficult, though, please feel free to leave this activity and come back to it. For many of us, there is a lot of grief and trauma around our inner children. If getting in touch with yours feels too painful, then it's fine to get support doing this work or wait until it feels doable for you. The emotional thermometer from Chapter 11 might help you to judge when it feels a good time for you to do an activity like this.

My inner child/ren

As we've said, we also often disown anything that's seen as unacceptable for us by wider society or by the people around us. For example, if we were viewed as "the one who needs looking after" in our family, we might have disowned strength and power. If we were viewed as "the ray of sunshine," we may have disowned any sides of us which struggled or found things difficult or upsetting. If our wider community said it was important for people to be humble and "not get above themselves," then we might have disowned confidence and cockiness. If it told us that we needed to be frightened of others, then we might have come to view ourselves as a coward and disowned the sides of us which were brave or confrontational.

Because these sides of us are disowned, when we don't know them, we may end up looking for others who embody them, or projecting them on to other people and judging them for it. These sides of us may also end up leaking out or exploding at times, surprising or shocking us and the people around us. This gives us a clue to a couple of useful ways of identifying our disowned selves.

What kinds of people are you drawn to in others—either real people in your life or celebrities or fictional characters? Could it be that they represent aspects of yourself that you're not in touch with (disowned selves) or which you are (foregrounded selves)?

. . . .

. . . .

. . . .

. . . .

What kinds of people do you find yourself judging or being repelled by—either real people in your life or celebrities or fictional characters. Could it be that they represent aspects of yourself that you're not in touch with (disowned selves) or which you are (foregrounded selves)?

. . . .

. . . .

. . . .

. . . .

What characteristics do you *love* people seeing in you and/or commenting on? Could it be that this represents aspects of yourself that you're not in touch with (disowned selves) or which you are (foregrounded selves)?

. . . .

. . . .

. . . .

. . . .

What characteristics do you *hate* people seeing in you and/or commenting on? Could it be that this represents aspects of yourself that you're not in touch with (disowned selves) or which you are (foregrounded selves)?

. . . .

. . . .

. . . .

. . . .

You can also reflect on the relationships and situations in your life which you most enjoy—and most struggle with—and whether these point to the sides of you you're most comfortable being, and the sides you really dislike being.

It's important—as always—to be gentle with yourself when exploring your disowned selves because they can be frightening and unfamiliar when we've pushed them down for so long. Again, kind self-care is a vital cradle for this more reflective work, and it's fine to get support from others, including therapists or spiritual practitioners who specialize in this kind of work.

Before we go on, here is a list of lots of different practices you can use for identifying your different selves—foregrounded and disowned. You might like to pick one of these to try and then reflect on how that was for you. Remember that different practices work for different people, and at different times in their lives. Often, it's great to work with one that is the kind of thing you already do—for example, writing if you keep a journal, or moving your body to music if that's something you enjoy already.

Art and craft: It can be useful to draw your selves as characters or as more abstract shapes and colors. There's no need to be "artistic." You can also model the selves using Lego or Plasticine, or pick stones, buttons, toys or other objects to represent them. Pick one that captures each self, and put them in relation to each other if that works. You could move them around to how you'd like them to be in relation to each other. You could draw mind maps or landscape-style maps if you'd rather.

Collages and playlists: It can be great to create collages, scrapbooks, pinterest boards or playlists of tunes for each self. This can be anything that you associate with that energy: celebrities, animals, lyrics, characters, colors, weather, mythical creatures, tarot cards, drinks, food, clothes, times of year, genres, TV shows and so on.

Body and movement: It can be great to learn how each self feels in your body. You can try moving, standing or sitting, in postures that bring each one to the fore. Dancing in each self—or between them—can work well, especially if you associate different music with them. Different selves can also be brought out by different physical activities such as swimming, working out, curling up in bed, washing or cuddling. If meditation works for you, you can just sit and bring a self to mind, experiencing how it is in your body when you're with the felt sense of it (see Chapter 11).

Try one of these ideas and reflect on how it was for you.

CHAPTER 19

Caring for—and Communicating Between—Your Plural Selves

Once you have a sense of some of your plural selves, it can be great to start communicating with—and between—them. The idea here is to get to know each of them and improve the lines of communication between them so that they're more able to work together.

This is all a constant journey—or work in progress. It may be that as you get to know your selves, and improve communication between them, more selves emerge, or you realize that some are different facets of the same self. It may be that you reach more nuanced understandings of the roles that certain selves had in your life. The different selves may face difficult challenges and/or grow and change. For example, MJ found that their warrior-protector self was also the most controlling part and needed to be supported to let go of having to be in charge all the time.

A good starting point for communication can be to interview each self either from a kind of neutral voice or from one or other of your selves. Below is a list of potential questions you might ask. Choose the ones that feel most applicable for you and feel free to add to them. You can do the interviews in writing, out loud (recorded if you want to), in your imagination, or whatever feels best to you. Just try to answer the questions from a particular part of yourself: whichever feels most present, perhaps.

- What is your defining trait?

- What are your superpowers?

- What is your shadow side, major flaw, Achilles heel or kryptonite?

- What do you want?

- What do you need?

- What do you offer me/us as a whole?

- Where did you come from?

- When in my life did you come forward or get pushed down?

- What situations and relationships bring you out?

- What blocks you from functioning well?

- What would you do if you were in control?

- What helps you to grow?

We often try to limit ourself to one self, or at least only the selves that are approved of by others. Self-monitoring involves attempting to police our selves so that only certain ones are revealed to others, and even to ourself. We've seen how many of us develop a strong "inner critic" and/or "controller" self, which does this policing and keeps "unacceptable" selves hidden. When selves we are highly uncomfortable with emerge, we may try to eradicate them. Or we may feel horribly stuck in them, and in the realization that this is someone we can be, and want to destroy ourselves completely. For example, we might find ourselves being the lecherous drunk or the scared little boy, the enraged bull or the callous manipulator.

An alternative to avoiding or trying to battle these different sides of ourselves is to be open to all the selves that we are, to cultivate awareness of them and good communication between them. This can be extremely difficult when it comes to the selves we're scared of or disgusted by. However, paradoxically, when we face them and listen to them, rather than trying to block them up on the other side of a high brick wall, we often find that they're less terrifying and overwhelming than we feared.

Some approaches view the goal of plural work as integrating our selves into a singular self, or at least creating a leader self who is in control. We find these problematic approaches, based as they are on a dominant culture perspective that people should be singular and consistent and coherent rather than plural and complex, and that systems should be hierarchies rather than collectives.

We prefer the model of our plural selves as a team or crew, each part of which has different strengths and limitations and works best when they're in good communication with each other. Like a team, collective or the crew of a ship, the group generally has largely shared goals and may be heading in roughly the same direction, but it is composed of different selves which have quite different qualities and capacities. Some characters in it are more dominant than others. In each relationship or situation, one or more selves may come to the fore and others go more into the background. Vital to this is the capacity to communicate together, to flow between different selves, and to commit to no leaders or controllers, and no casting out or eradicating of certain selves.

Try sketching the plural selves you've identified so far below as the crew of a sailing ship. You might want to locate them in different parts of the ship and think about who takes various roles (captain, mate, crow's nest look-out, cook, crew member who challenges everyone, etc.). If that metaphor doesn't work for you, feel free to pick another one (e.g. lands on a map, characters in a sitcom, members of a superhero team, colleagues in a workplace, crew of a starship).

My crew

If you find that your crew is not in great communication at the moment, you might want to do another sketch of how you'd rather your ship (or other metaphor) looked. For example, you might have a large captain or controller who is steering the ship into dangerous waters. What would it look like if they took a different role and somebody else was steering? What about if they were listening better to everybody else?

My crew as a collective

One useful way to balance things, and to identify more of our disowned selves, is to consider which characteristics we foreground and what might be the counter to that.

For example, you might consider your foregrounded selves and what would be useful balances to each of them like in the example that follows.

Foregrounded self	Balancing disowned self
Critic	Nurturing compassion
People-pleaser	Cocky self-belief
Perfectionist	Playful self who is happy doing nothing

You can deliberately try communicating with these balancing selves, learning who they might be. It's not about going from one extreme to the other, but learning how to hear from both/all sides. It can be really helpful to ask, "What would you do in this situation?" or, "What would you do if you were in control?" to both sides of the balance. This can open up new ideas and possibilities.

Perhaps the most obvious way of bringing our selves into communication is dialogue between them. We can do this in many different ways, such as:

- Journaling or writing down the dialogue like a script between two characters.

- Using the "empty chair" technique where we set out two chairs or cushions and move between them talking as first one self and then the other.

- Imagining the two selves as characters in our minds and having an internal conversation.

- Going on a walk somewhere and having an out-loud conversation between two selves. It may help to move from one side of the path to the other, turning our head different ways, in order to embody the two selves. It may be good to go somewhere where there aren't many people and/or to put headphones in, as if you were on the phone, if you're worried about other people's responses.

- Lying in bed and talking between two selves last thing at night to debrief the day—either as an external or internal conversation.

- Having a therapist—or friend who is also doing this kind of work—facilitating a dialogue between two or more of your selves as they move between seats, like family therapy.

You might pick whichever selves feel most live to talk between, or two that represent different extremes (e.g. serious and playful, emotional and rational), or two that have different ideas about what choice you should make, one who needs support and another who has support to offer, or you can try talking between more than two selves at once, or checking in with the whole team (or part of it).

Dreams, fantasies and fiction provide another possible way of communicating between our selves. There is a theory that all elements of night dreams, daydreams and fantasies represent different sides of us. You can write down your dreams and fantasies and consider what the different characters/elements present were, and whether they might represent your different selves. It can be interesting to do a similar thing with the fictional characters in a show, book or movie you enjoy as well.

Daydreams, fantasies and fiction can also become a way to deliberately bring your selves into communication—if your imagination works that way. For example:

- Write a short story about two of your selves as characters, perhaps about their first meeting, or them being stuck in a lift together, going on a date, or finding themselves washed up on a desert island.

- Imagine, or draw, a big house—or other landscape—for all your selves. Give each one a room and decorate it, making spaces for them to go to when they're struggling, or want to get together in communal spaces.

- Have romantic or erotic fantasies between different selves, if that feels appropriate for you.

- Make a comic or cartoon of an exchange between two or more selves.

Try one of these ideas and reflect on how it was for you.

Something that we've returned to again and again in this workbook is the idea that self-care is difficult—if not impossible—without daily rhythms and rituals to support it, and without systems and structures of support. So how might we access rhythms and rituals, and systems and structures, to support our plural selves work?

Supportive rhythms and rituals

Thinking back to Chapter 8, if you work with plural selves, you can deliberately design an altar to reflect those selves, perhaps with objects that you can move around to represent some/all of them. You can also develop rituals, like the ones described in Chapter 8, to specifically explore, or communicate between, your selves.

You might find it helpful to consider what daily practices bring out different selves, and to keep thinking about the balance of your days in order to ensure that different ones are brought forward at different times. For example, certain selves may excel at "just being" or may enjoy moving their body or may come out when you're stimulating your mind or doing soothing activities, or practical ones.

It can also be useful and playful to develop rituals to communicate between selves. For example, MJ enjoys doing a "secret santa" approach to birthdays where they put each self's name in a hat and pull them out on behalf of other selves. Each self then makes or buys another a gift and/or draws or writes a card. If you have a lot of selves, you could just do this between some of them, or between groups of selves.

What plural rhythms and rituals might you experiment with?

Supportive systems and structures

This kind of work can be hard to do alone, and sadly there is still a lot of stigma and misunderstanding around people experiencing themselves as plural, especially for those of us where our experience of plurality is vivid and/or we dissociate between different selves.

In addition to therapists who specialize in this area (e.g. psychosynthesis, internal family systems, gestalt, transactional analysis, subpersonalities), it can be useful to develop supportive networks of friends who are doing similar work, or tap into existing networks such as the Plural Positivity community.

We can intentionally cultivate relationships in our lives which draw out different selves or characteristics as part of balancing these. Part of intentional relationships may be chatting in our friendships and other close relationships about which sides of us are drawn out in those relationships, which ones we'd like to share more and how to do that, and which sides may not work so well in those relationships. There will be more about intentional relationships in Chapter 21.

We hope we've made it clear that this can be deep work, even though it can also be fun, playful, creative and helpful. Do get any support you need around it, especially if it gets scary or overwhelming. There's no rush. Take it at your own pace. There are several more books and websites to support this work listed in the further resources at the end of this workbook.

∞

CHAPTER 20

Caring for Your
Ever-Changing Self/Selves

This is the section of the workbook in which we're going to get a bit sci-fi. In Chapter 17, we introduced the idea that as well as understanding ourself as plural, we might understand ourself as fluid or constantly changing. This means that we can also be in relationship with our selves past, present and future.

When we see ourself as something static that we could pin down and always be, we limit and constrain ourselves. Therapist Manu Bazzano says it's like taking a bowl to the river, filling it with water and then looking into the bowl to understand the river (2016). Really, we *are* the river, ever flowing and always in process.

Let's take a look at your own river of experience. Sketch a bending river on the next page, perhaps all the way from the source to the sea. You can start at any point in your life, but we suggest starting from birth or your early memories. You can finish at any point too, perhaps now or maybe you'd like to imagine ahead to the future, or even to death or beyond. Your river can just be a line across the page or as rich a drawing as you want to make it. Don't overthink it.

Each bend in the river is a significant moment that led you to your understanding of yourself (or selves) today. Each bend is a person, event, book, movie, song, encounter, object—anything really that significantly influenced your self as it is today.

Draw your river slowly, annotating each bend with a few keywords or images, to remind you what each bend represents. Once you've drawn your river, reflect on where you were in relationship to each bend. Were you in the river? If so, were you swimming comfortably, on a boat, or struggling to keep afloat? Were you sitting by the edge watching your river flow by?

Please remember to be gentle with yourself as you go through this activity, and take your time to breathe and have breaks as needed. For this, and the following activities, please remember that it's OK if you don't have much memory of some—or all—times in your life. Trauma and dissociation, different cognitive capacities and neurodiversities mean that people have very different recollections of the past from none to total recall, and everything in between. As always, if this is hard for you, then do get support—for example, from a trauma-informed therapist. If it just doesn't click or work for you, feel free to leave it and go on to Chapter 21.

For another version of this activity, imagine that your life is a book. What does the contents page look like? Write a list of the chapters of your life. You can start at any point in the past that feels right, and end in the present or the future. It's up to you. If you're not into books, you might think about the different acts or scenes in a movie, the different tracks on an album or the levels of a computer game.

Me

You can then reflect on what you've written.

- Where did you start?

- Where did you end?

- What kind of book/movie/album/game would yours be?

- What genre? Are there any major themes?

- Who's the primary author?

- What would it look like if someone else in your life wrote it?

- Is there any part of your life missing from it?

- How would it look if you focused on that instead?

- Who'd be the most appreciative audience, or the most critical one?

- What would it be called?

So we can understand our self—or selves—as in progress rather than static and fixed. In fact, there are many different stories we could tell through our lives. Again, we might get stuck on one particular narrative, but it can be useful to open that up.

Psychologist Kenneth Gergen (2001) suggests that we tell stories to make sense of our lives, often starting from a particular endpoint: how I came to be X, where X could be anything from a doctor to a gambler, a dad to a divorcee, a liberal to a long-distance runner. We keep editing and repeating certain stories to ourselves over time so they come to feel like a solid truth.

Popular narratives include:

- *The tragedy*—where we start in a successful place, but fall into failure.

- *The comedy-romance*—where a positive life is interrupted by calamity, but order is restored.

- *The happily-ever-after*—when things get gradually better and better.

- *The heroic narrative*—where we struggle towards victory against a number of obstacles, but eventually win out.

What would your story look like if you started from a different endpoint, or used a different narrative structure?

Sociologist Ken Plummer (2002) points out that new stories, or at least variations on old ones, emerge in our culture over time, such as the "coming-out story" or the "victim narrative." Again, these stories might be very useful in terms of making sense of our lives, but it's also good not to get so stuck in them that they restrict our future.

If you have a "coming-out" narrative, what might your life story look like if you focused on a different aspect of your identity? If you've been a victim, can you also tell stories through parts of your life as a rescuer, a hero, a survivor or even a persecutor?

Narrative therapists would invite you to think about what your preferred stories might be. Once you've identified those preferred stories, you could take some time to flesh them out by imagining them in more detail. You might also think about recruiting an audience for your preferred stories. Who will you share those stories with? Who can be good allies in your preferred stories?

When we have a sense of our life over time we can get even more sci-fi and experiment with time-traveling.

Again, a self-care heads-up—this can be deep work, especially if we travel back to difficult or traumatic times in our lives. When MJ first heard about this practice, they tried to make a list of all the times they wanted to travel back to, and ended up re-traumatizing themself and being in bad shape for a good few weeks. Remember to go gently. Remember to keep checking in with your emotion thermometer. Remember to access support if and when needed. Trauma-informed therapists can help support you to do time-travel visualizations if it feels risky to do these alone.

Sarah Peyton's (2017) neuroscience book and audio *Your Resonant Self* gives several guided meditations for time-traveling back to visit past selves. The idea is that tough memories can stay very live and vivid in our minds, but if we revisit them safely, it's possible to shift them out of the present and into longer-term storage, so they don't loom so large or impact our present so much.

Sarah Peyton suggests cultivating a gentle, kind, witness side of yourself who can accompany you back to situations in the past. If you work with plural selves, you can also experiment with going back as a team, or taking a side of yourself who is likely to be particularly supportive in that situation.

Some ways you might practice time-traveling include:

- Trying some of the guided meditations in *Your Resonant Self*, or similar books/audios.

- Sitting with your eyes closed and remembering back to a past memory that you want to revisit. Beginning with one that comes up for you every now and then, but doesn't feel too painful or overwhelming, is a good starting point. Perhaps try a niggling encounter that happened recently to start with. When you get back, run through what happened in your mind, if that works for you. You could imagine it playing out on a TV, for example. Then you can rewind, pause, fast-forward, or anything else that's useful. We've found it helpful sometimes to replace ourselves in the memory with somebody else—a character or person we admire, for example—to see how they respond. We can also imagine that character as a bystander and think how they might intervene in the situation. We can imagine them as a witness supporting us. We can replace the other person or people and imagine how somebody we admire might have responded differently. When we feel as if we're done with the memory, we can talk with our past self about how they're doing now and—if they want—we can bring them back into the present with us.

- Journaling a conversation with a past self in a similar way that you would with plural selves, described in Chapter 19, or talking with them out loud.

- Creating a comic of a past memory and—if you like—include your present self—or gentle witness—coming in to help, support, or console that past version of you.

- You can create playlists, collages or temporary altars for past selves in order to get back in touch with those times in your life and develop kindness for them.

- Write letters back to past versions of you, forward to future versions of you, and reply from those versions if you fancy it. You might make a pen pal.

Now we've opened up to the sci-fi world of multiple stories and time-traveling, we can also consider parallel universes. Some people find it helpful to imagine different versions of themselves living different sliding-door lives, perhaps having made different decisions at pivotal points in their lives.

Again, cultivating kindness for these parallel selves, and communicating between them to learn from each other in the kinds of ways we've explored here, can be useful. Whether we are communicating with plural selves, past selves, parallel selves or future selves, such conversations can be a helpful way to access different wisdoms which we're not always in touch with, or seeing our lives more fully or from a different perspective.

You might find the idea of past, present and future selves helpful for relating with yourself on a more everyday basis. When past you did something that made life easier for present you, can you remember to take time to express gratitude towards them? Can you cultivate faith in future you so that you can give present you more of a break? For example, at the end of the day we often feel overwhelmed and as if we don't have much more to give. Can you get in the habit of thinking "I know future me will have this, so it's OK to rest now?" When you're in crisis or sick, can you remember past crises and sickness passing, and trust that a future version of yourself will be back on their feet and more able to cope?

Can you use that remembering to support present you to rest and recuperate, not trying to do anything until they feel ready?

As with plural selves (Chapters 18 and 19), it's useful to build in regular rhythms and rituals, as well as systems and structures, to support work with ourself in process over time. It might be useful here to go back to the end of Chapter 19 and consider how you might build in everyday—or regular—rituals and routines to support working with your past, present and future selves, as well as how you might cultivate communities of support around this work.

Rhythms and rituals to support myself-in-process

. . . .

. . . .

. . . .

. . . .

Systems and structures to support myself-in-process

. . . .

. . . .

. . . .

. . . .

Over the next four chapters, we'll turn to our relationships with others in more detail and continue to explore how we can cultivate systems and structures of support for our self-/other-care.

M.Y.O. Slow Down Page

How do your selves want to slow down?

P.S. It's OK if different parts of you need different things.

Self-Care and Other-Care

CHAPTER 21

We Are in Relationship All the Time

Throughout this workbook, we've talked about how we cannot take care of ourselves in isolation. We're part of systems, such as families, cultures, communities and so on. Our relationships with these systems shape our capacity to care for ourselves and others. Some cultures are more individual based and others more community based. This too is a spectrum, with varying degrees of emphasis on individual or community. For example, MJ comes from an Anglo culture, which is usually more individual based, whereas Alex comes from Italy, which is generally more community based, especially in the south. However, Alex now lives in the US, which has a very individualistic culture, and their oldest child is tri-cultural—she has the two cultures she was born and brought up in (English and Italian) and has lived in the US since she was four years old.

This means that, even though we believe that we're in relationship all the time—both within ourselves, as explored in the previous four chapters, and with others, as expressed repeatedly throughout the book—we might think about relationships in a range of ways. This might be a good time to think about what culture(s) you were brought up in and which culture you live in now. Those might be different or the same, of course.

First, take time to notice the messages that you received about relationships growing up. Were individual needs placed above community needs or vice versa? Did you learn one message at home and a different one at school, or through popular culture, such as TV shows, comics, books and so on?

Now think about the culture(s) you may be immersed in currently... Is it a more individualistic- or community-based culture? Are you immersed in different cultures? If so, do these cultures share values about individuals and community or do they have different values?

Finally, take time to think about your own values. Do you tend to think more in individual- or community-based ways? What impact does this have on people around you? Are your values in line with those of the dominant culture you live in, or not? If they are, how do you benefit from sharing those values? If not, how are you and those around you impacted by this difference?

No matter which culture(s) we might come from, we're in relationship all the time. Our relationships are not just with people but also with place, language, plants, animals, history, ancestors and so on. How does being relational beings impact our capacity to care for ourselves and one another? How do we balance caring for ourselves and others? These are some of the questions we'll explore together in this chapter and the following three.

Even though we're immersed in relationships all the time, our experience is that sometimes this can feel overwhelming. For example, we might feel pulled in different directions at the same time: one way is what we want to do for ourselves and the other way is what other people need. If we experience ourselves as plural or fluid, we might even feel that push and pull internally!

This is where the metaphor of relationships as a dance has been useful, at least for us. When we're dancing, we don't always have the same energy or feel drawn to the same rhythms or people. Sometimes we might want to slow-dance by ourselves, or with another person. Other times, we might want to dance fast, as if nobody was watching. Other times still, we might find joy in a group dance, in which our moves are synchronous. We might enjoy mirroring one another when dancing, or not. We might enjoy listening to music as we dance or dance to our own inner beat, and so on.

If we think of relationships as dance, we can also think of times when our internal music does not match with what the radio or the DJ is playing. We can think of times when finding people who enjoy dancing as much as we do has been joyous and freed us to take up space on the dance floor. Dance is fluid. We're expected to move at different rhythms and tempos. Some of us might be more familiar with some steps than others. The joy comes from moving, whether alone or with others. We might feel more or less comfortable with one or the other, but it doesn't make one "good" or "bad," "better" or "worse."

When we think about relationships in this way, we find it a little easier to imagine how we might be able to take care of both ourselves and other people. It becomes a little easier to move from self-focus on care to other-focus, and even to have both happen at the same time, if we're both enjoying dancing to the same music.

Let's apply this metaphor to an exercise. Think about three to five relationships in your life. These could be with people, but also with animal companions, possibility role models, fictional characters, plants and so on. Once you have thought about them, fill in their names in the table on the next page, in the left-hand column.

Then create a mini-playlist for each of these relationships. This could be three to six songs or pieces of music. Once you have created all the playlists, take your time to explore them. Imagine the relationship you're exploring, play the playlist and move! As you do this, what sensations, emotions, thoughts, images or memories come up for you? How does it feel to move to the rhythms of that particular playlist? Once you have explored one playlist thoroughly, you might want to try another. What happens this time? What do you notice? Are there differences between your experience from one playlist to another? You can even move with one of the people, animal companions or plants on your list, if it feels safe enough to do so. Does that change your experience? Take note of what you have learned, if anything, and remember that this is an exercise you can come back to as often as you want.

Relationship	Playlist

Why would we encourage you to dance, literally and metaphorically, with the various relationships in your life? As well as recognizing that we're connected, interdependent beings, we believe that being able to identify which relationships nourish us, which deplete us, which do both, and every stage in between, is essential to our self-care.

How do we know when to stretch because a beloved is in crisis or community is in upheaval, and when we need to retreat for a moment or two—or longer—to take care of ourselves? How do we know which relationships to set boundaries with, and how (more on this in the next couple of pages)? How do we learn to acknowledge the shifts and changes that happen within our relationships over time? Do we know when to adjust course, when to renegotiate expectations, hopes and dreams and so on?

All of this can be challenging. Just as Anglo and Western dominant cultures seem to view the self as fixed and immutable, they seem to view relationships in this way too. However, we know from experience that relationships rarely stay the same. Even when commitments might endure, people grow, change, get sick, find new passions, or the world simply changes around us.

Recognizing how we impact relationships and how we're impacted by them is crucial to being able to stay in relationship with the world around us. Another way of looking at our relationships, besides nourishment and depletion, which might seem a very capitalist and transactional model in some ways, is to ask ourselves what they open up and what they close down. For example, the writing partnership that we—this book's authors—have opens up the potential for more creation, books, podcast episodes, presentations and so on. It also opens up to further intimacy over time. We've discovered that we're good traveling companions, for example. In other ways, it closes down opportunities to just hang out sometimes, without a material goal, or to wander and wonder within the relationship itself.

The point we're trying to make here is that all relationships are a "yes" to something and a "no" to something else, an opening up and a closing down, and they can both nourish us and deplete us in a range of ways. So take a moment to consider your relationships, right now. Maybe you want to pick a few, or even just one. Give yourself time to consider how you impact the relationship(s) and how you're impacted. What's opening up and/or closing down in your life because of this—or these—relationship(s)? Which relationships are nourishing, depleting or a bit of both? Have they changed over time? Take time to note down your answers on the next page by writing, drawing or whatever else works for you.

So what we do once we've recognized how we impact relationships and how we're impacted by them? One of the things we invite you to do is to consider whether your boundaries are where you want them to be, both for yourself and in the various relationships in your life. It might seem counterintuitive to talk about boundaries in a chapter that's all about us being in relationships all the time. However, we truly believe that boundaries help us stay in healthy relationships with one another. So let's back up and talk about what boundaries are in the first place.

Boundaries are the way we communicate what's OK, what's not OK and what might be negotiable in some circumstances. They are our yes, no and maybe. Sophia Graham, a relationship coach and author of the blog *Love Uncommon*, writes in one of her posts about a metaphor for boundaries that she learned from counselor Diana Ryan. Diana talked about boundaries in relation to what our home would look like depending on our boundaries and our upkeep of those boundaries. Does that image resonate for you?

Sophia goes on to describe her own challenges with boundaries and going from a house with poor boundaries, such as fences in disrepair, to a fortress of solitude with barbed wire and high walls, which was also not helping her stay in healthy relationships with others. Ultimately, healthy boundaries are firm and solid but not impenetrable! We do want to be able to let some people in and not others, to ask people to leave and come back, or leave and never come back. The job of boundaries is to help us stay connected, not to keep us so safe that we're ultimately incredibly lonely and isolated.

As always, culture has a lot to do with how we might feel about boundaries, and which boundaries we might consider appropriate and reasonable or inappropriate and unreasonable. For example, in some cultures there is an expectation that people will give one another a certain amount of space in public, whereas in others there is no such expectation. Boundaries also vary from situation to situation and we're likely to have different boundaries with different people.

We can make some generalizations around categories that boundaries tend to fall into—that is, rigid, porous and healthy. However, the same boundary could be considered healthy by someone and rigid by someone else, depending on cultural and community expectations. Usually, rigid boundaries are not at all flexible. People with rigid boundaries tend to isolate, be self-sufficient and very private, not ask for help, and might come across as distant. People with porous boundaries tend often to be people-pleasers, have challenges with saying "no," value other people's opinions, often above their own, and try to avoid rejection by doing what other people want, or what they think they want. This might lead them to stay in relationships with abusive patterns. Finally, people with healthy boundaries tend to be clear on their own values; they know what they want and don't want, can communicate this to others, and can easily accept other people saying "no" to them.

As we said, we all tend to have those traits at one point or another in our lives, and in some relationships or situations. Do you recognize yourself in any, some or all of the descriptions above? If so, what is your reaction to seeing your boundaries reflected in those categories? Try to engage with your thoughts and feelings with as much curiosity, non-judgment and kindness as you're able.

If you're finding it difficult to set boundaries, you might want to try the following exercise. Take a moment to list your top five values in relationships. You may want to look at the core values exercise in Chapter 7. Do these essential, defining values still stand when you look at them through a relational lens, or would you like to pick some different ones, or mix and match?

My five top values in relationships are:

1

2

3

4

5

Now take some time to think about what works for you in relationships and what does not. You can use the space below to annotate your thoughts. You might want to do this part several times. For example, you might want to think of your close friendships or work relationships or family relationships or romantic relationships or sexual relationships or creative relationships and so on—you get the idea!

What works for me in [insert type of relationship here] is:

For example, Alex would say here that people understanding that their energy and capacity for doing things can shift and change, because of their disability, works in all their relationships.

. . . .

. . . .

What doesn't work for me in [insert type of relationship here] is:

For example, Alex would say here that someone being "pushy" about doing things when they don't have energy would not work for them in any relationships.

. . . .

. . . .

Now take time to consider your values in relationships, what works and what doesn't work, and try to write down or say out loud some boundaries you'd like to set or express in any of your relationships.

Following from the examples above, Alex might say here that they will not stay in close relationships with people who can't hear their no, or who get upset at changing plans because of health reasons

. . . .

. . . .

CHAPTER 22

Caring for Ourselves and Others:
Interconnection and Interdependence

We've mentioned in the previous chapter how caring for ourselves and others can feel like being pulled in different directions at times. Are self and other in opposition, or even separate? As we mentioned in one of our previous books, *Life Isn't Binary* (2019), binary ways of thinking about and doing relationships tend to exacerbate the binary between ourselves and another person.

Black feminist writer bell hooks and others have pointed out that love is simply not possible in a relationship where the self is valued far more highly than the other, or vice versa. What we have, under these conditions, is a tendency to treat the other person as an object or prop for our own benefit, by trying to make them into what we want them to be. Or we have the tendency to treat ourselves as an object or prop for somebody else's benefit, by trying to shape ourselves into their ideal.

Take some time to think about this in your own relationships. Are there times when you value yourself over the other person? Are there times when you value the other person over yourself? What happens when you do one or the other? You might want to consider relationship conflicts in particular (we'll talk more about conflict later). What would it look like to value yourself and the other person equally at such times?

What boundaries would you need to feel that both you and other people can value both your own and each other's wellbeing? Are there relationships in your life that feel mutual—that is, you feel you both give and receive? If not, what gets in the way? Do you tend to give in relationships most of the time, or receive? If so, what are the obstacles that get in the way of your ability to both give and receive?

Note below any reflections or insights from your own life, remembering that some of these obstacles might be systemic, such as intergenerational patterns or cultural messages about what relationships are supposed to be like. As ever, please remember to go slow and be kind and gentle with yourself.

In *Life Isn't Binary,* we mentioned the Indigenous concept of decolonial love and it seems important to bring it back here as well. Decolonial love invites us to imagine love with consent and care for self and others at the heart. In this type of love, a critical reflection on power dynamics is ongoing, and there is a deep and continuing commitment to never non-consensually treat another person— or yourself—as property that somebody is entitled to in terms of a particular kind of relationship, or form of labour, that is expected.

This type of love is rooted in interdependence, which, by its nature, does not lend itself easily to hierarchies. Critical disability studies and Indignous studies, alongside black feminist scholarship, have highlighted how the independent/ dependent binary is unhelpful and incorrect, given that we are interdependent. Interdependence reminds us that we are connected, not just to other humans but also to the broader ecosystem. Many spiritual traditions, such as Buddhism, to which we refer often in this workbook, also challenge the idea of separation— or even the existence—of the individualized self.

Interdependence is not just a philosophical or metaphorical connection, but a very real one. To illustrate this, let's take a moment to do a brief activity from disability studies (Mason 1990). Imagine the first 15 minutes of your day after you wake up. Then list all the activities you do during that time. *For example, lying in bed listening to the radio, after turning the alarm clock down.*

Activities during the first 15 minutes after waking up:

. . . .

. . . .

. . . .

Now try to calculate how many people made those 15 minutes possible. If we go with the example given earlier, you might want to think about how many people were involved in making your alarm clock, or phone if this is what you use as an alarm clock. Then how many people were involved in making it possible for you to have a radio or stream a radio channel through a speaker? Also, how many people were involved in making the bed you lie on? How about the sheets? What about the electricity involved in powering your clock, phone or radio? How many people did that take?

How many people do you estimate were involved in making your first 15 minutes possible?

. . . .

This is what we mean when we say that interdependence is not just a metaphor or a philosophical construct. We all depend on one another to make our lives possible. We all depend on one another in varying degrees. We also increasingly depend on various forms of technology, and we depend on nature to power said technology, as well as to feed ourselves. We're not islands, and the labour of care is happening all the time. Sometimes that care work is recognized and sometimes it's taken for granted instead.

It's impossible to talk about care for ourselves and others without talking about disability justice. Well, we're sure it is possible, actually, but it's not something we're interested in. First of all, as author Leah Lakshmi Piepzna-Samarasinha (2018) records in the book *Care Work: Dreaming Disability Justice*, we want to acknowledge that:

> "Disability justice" is a term coined by the Black, brown, queer, and trans members of the original Disability Justice Collective, founded in 2005 by Patty Berne, Mia Mingus, Stacey Milbern, Leroy Moore, Eli Clare, and Sebastian Margaret. Disabled queer and trans Black, Asian, and white activists and artists, they dreamed up a movement-building framework that would center the lives, needs, and organizing strategies of disabled queer and trans and/or Black and brown people marginalized from mainstream disability rights organizing's white-dominated, single-issue focus. (p.17)

In the same book, Leah also reminds us that, for disabled people, accessing care is not a neutral or apolitical endeavor, and that it can be scary for people to admit the level of care they need. As she writes:

> People's fear of accessing care didn't come out of nowhere. It came out of generations and centuries where needing care meant being locked up, losing your human and civil rights, and being subject to abuse. (p.47)

When we talk about caring for ourselves and others, about interdependence, we're rooted in a disability justice framework and plugged into a larger liberatory framework. These are the histories we're connecting to. One final quote from Leah's book highlights just how close those connections between liberation movements are:

When we do disability justice work, it becomes impossible to look at disability and not examine how colonialism created it. It becomes a priority to look at Indigenous ways of perceiving and understanding disability, for example. It becomes a space where we see that disability is all up in Black and brown/ queer and trans communities—from Henrietta Lacks to Harriet Tubman, from the Black Panther Party's active support for disabled organizers' two-month occupation of the Department of Vocational Rehabilitation to force the passage of Section 504, the law mandating disabled access to public spaces and transportation to the chronic illness and disability stories of second-wave queer feminists of color like Sylvia Rivera, June Jordan, Gloria Anzaldúa, Audre Lorde, Marsha P. Johnson, and Barbara Cameron, whose lives are marked by bodily difference, trauma-surviving brilliance, and chronic illness but who mostly never used the term "disabled" to refer to themselves. (p.27)

When we talk about caring for ourselves and others, we're connecting to an invitation to a politics of relationship that never stopped, and that has always resisted colonial, dehumanizing and othering approaches to community and life. These politics of relationship are Indigenous, black, brown, disabled, immigrant, trans and queer. They are politics of resistance, survival and care. We're part of an ecosystem that is large, vibrant, adaptable and interdependent.

What does that all mean, then, for us, in our everyday lives? Remember all those messages we received about care that might get in the way of us being able to take care of ourselves and one another? When we see how large that web is, how we could never have been without our ancestors, not just of blood but also of activism, spirituality, creativity and so on, then we think it's harder to deny ourselves and one another the care we need.

Caring for ourselves in this paradigm becomes caring for the gifts of all who have gone before us, and also caring for all the communities we're part of. The reverse is also true. When we tend to community, we're also tending to ourselves, because if one part of community suffers without support, we also suffer. When we become part of communities of *need* rather than *convenience*, as another beloved friend, author and healer, Susan Raffo, would say, then to care for community becomes indispensable, because we need our community and they need us.

That is a lot of words so far in this chapter! Let's take a break for an exercise. Take a moment to create a drawing, symbol, list or mind map of all the ways in which caring for your communities is a part of caring for yourself, and vice versa. For example, you might find that when you have reminded friends it's fine to cancel prior arrangements, you also feel more able to cancel when you need to. You may experience that being part of creating a community space also nourishes you as you hear from the people who come to be in that space with you.

One last thing we want to touch on in this chapter is our capacity to receive care. We know that for some of us it can be easier to give than to receive care. It can feel challenging to ask for what we need in a world that tells us that doing so is "weakness" or "failure" by colonial, capitalist, ableist standards.

For example, while writing this book, we negotiated our care needs. Alex had to state the inability to carry bags during this trip due to increased pain levels and decreased mobility. Even though MJ was more than happy to carry these bags, Alex still felt guilty and tried to offer to carry the shopping bags while grocery shopping! We understand how hard it can be to let ourselves receive care, even knowing that it's OK and that we deserve to receive care.

Receiving care is essential within a culture of interdependence. Both giving and receiving care are essential, but we want to highlight a side that we know many of us might struggle with: *receiving*.

Take a moment to write down all the ways in which you could receive care. You can also draw a mind map, make a collage or whatever works for you.

Now look at the list, mind map or collage and take time to reflect on whether you ask for those care needs to be met. When and where do you let yourself receive care? Who do you ask for care from? Are there care needs that go unmet because you have not been able to ask for what you need? What gets in the way of you being able to receive care? Take a moment to note any reflections or insights.

CHAPTER 23

Cultivating Consensual and Intentional Relationships

Part of seeing ourselves as interconnected and interdependent is recognizing that care is relational rather than individual. Although "self-care" is the common phrase to describe treating ourselves in a kind, caring manner, perhaps relational care, community care or interconnected care would be better phrases to capture the fact that we're always in relation, and that care for ourselves is intrinsically interwoven with care for others.

In this chapter, we focus on our interpersonal relationships, before turning to the communities and cultures around them in Chapter 24. How can we ensure that our close relationships support all of those within them to care for ourselves? By close relationships, here we're referring to the people you feel closest with. These may be friends, cohabiting relationships, partners of various kinds, logical or biological family, close colleagues or other kinds of relationships. Take a moment to note down the people, and other beings, in your life who you would describe as your close relationships.

. . . .

. . . .

. . . .

. . . .

. . . .

. . . .

This is who we're talking about here. Don't worry if you're not sure who this would be for you, as we'll talk more about finding your people and community in Chapter 24.

Close relationships can support the people within them to care for themselves and others or they can make this very difficult. For example, the people around us may model the kinds of practices we've covered in this workbook—taking time off when they're sick, being clear about what they can offer and where their limits are, being kind towards themselves in words and deeds, noticing when they're overstretched and making time for rest and retreat. If we see them do these things, we may well find it easier to do the same ourselves—to treat ourselves, and them, in a caring manner. However, if people around us are highly self-critical and always pushing themselves, comparing themselves to others and judging, blaming and shaming, we may find it very difficult not to be drawn into such ways of relating ourselves.

Similarly, the expectations that people in our lives have of us may make it easier—or more difficult—for us to care for ourselves and for them. For example, if others expect us to overstep our boundaries to look after them, to keep relationship secrets and not access outside support, to put their needs before our own, or to stay with them in situations that aren't safe for us, this may be detrimental to our self-care and—paradoxically—to our capacity to be good for them. However, self- and other-care may be easier if they make it their business to help us to know—and state—our limits, if they encourage us to get support outside the relationship and cultivate their own support networks, and if they value our wants and needs, limits and boundaries equally with theirs.

We can also cultivate relational self- and other-caring practices within our relationships, which make it easier for those in the relationships to be mutually kind and caring. In the rest of this chapter, we focus on two practices for doing this: consensual relating and intentional relationships.

Consent is a keyword when thinking about our relationships. As we said in Chapter 4—when we considered consent as one of the four supports for the cradle of kindness—consent is about helping everyone in a relationship to tune into their wants, needs, limits and boundaries, and to communicate openly about these.

Sadly, we all live in a highly non-consensual culture where other people often treat us less than consensually (as the #metoo movement highlighted) and where we're often encouraged to overstep our own self-consent. Think about how often friends pressurize each other to do social events that they don't fancy, or to drink or eat certain foods; partners push each other to spend certain kinds of time together, keep the house a certain way or prioritize the other person's goals or dreams; families make assumptions about the kind of contact they should have—or how they should spend the holidays—even though it may work well for nobody!

Similarly, when it comes to ourselves, we often push ourselves way past our limits and boundaries because we think we "should" work harder, get fitter, look different, act a certain way and so on. MJ had a classic moment of recognizing this when they started writing this chapter and realized they were forcing themselves to keep writing when they felt grumpy and tired, just because they'd hoped to get the chapter written today! It also took them several minutes to realize what was happening and to explain to Alex why they were struggling, meaning that Alex was pretty confused in the meantime. Even those of us who think all the time about consent struggle to treat ourselves—and others—consensually. This is understandable when we live in such a non-consensual culture.

One of our favourite bloggers, Sophia Graham, who we've mentioned before in this workbook, explains that many of us need to (re)learn what being in consent feels like because our consent has been overridden—by ourselves and others—throughout our lives. Think about how kids are often made to engage in physical contact they don't want, eat foods they don't like, and work on things they don't feel motivated about. And many of us have been through more abusive forms of non-consent such as school bullying and physical, sexual and/or emotional abuse or neglect within the home and/or in partner relationships.

Before we go on to explore how we can cultivate self-consent and consensual relationships, think about the elements of non-consent around for you growing up, and in the relationships, communities and cultures around you now. Make a few notes here. Obviously, this can be painful to think about, so please remember to be gentle with yourself, and skip this activity, if it feels too hard to reflect on right now.

. . . .

. . . .

. . . .

. . . .

. . . .

. . . .

. . . .

. . . .

. . . .

. . . .

Because of our non-consensual cultures and histories, Sophia and others have come up with practices to help us to learn what consent feels like in our bodies, and how to know what we feel like when our consent is being overridden by ourselves and others. Here are a couple of practices you might like to try. Do check out Sophia's *Love Uncommon* website, and Betty Martin's *The Wheel of Consent* website, if you'd like to find out more about these and other self-consent practices.

Yes and no lists (adapted from *Love Uncommon*)

Write two lists: one of things that feel like a big "yes" to you, and another of things that feel like a big "no." You might include flavours and scents you love and hate, animals, clothes, TV shows, music, places and experiences. Leave off anything that's traumatic for you, or related to a phobia or something else you really struggle with (e.g. food if you struggle around eating). When you have a bunch of ideas, make a top-seven list for yes and no.

Yes	No

The next part of the exercise helps you to learn how "yes" and "no" feel for you. You might want to do these at different times rather than one after the other. First, take a look at your "yes" list and pick something that jumps out. Write a short account of what that thing is for you and why you want to say "yes" to it. As you're writing, try to find the place in your body where you know that you enjoy it. Where do you feel the "yes"? It could be a sensation on your skin, or in your chest or belly. Wherever it is, find that place and recognize any emotions that go with that feeling. Find the words to describe them and write them down too. The feelings and somatic exercises from earlier in this workbook may help you. Feel free to do this for other items on your "yes" list to get a real sense of it. Then—or later—do the same for your "no" list.

Waking the hands (adapted from *The Wheel of Consent*)

Another activity, from Betty Martin, can help you to get an embodied sense of self-consent. Simply pick up an inanimate object that you like (a stone or an ornament, perhaps). Begin exploring the object with your hands and just notice it. What does it feel like? Is it hard or soft? Warm or cool? See if you can find a way of touching or stroking the object which feels pleasant or enjoyable for you. Maybe the heaviness is satisfying, or perhaps the softness is nice to press into. This helps you to experience what it feels like to go towards your "yes" without worrying about anybody else.

As already mentioned, the relationships around us can help to support us to be in self-consent or can make it difficult for us. It is hoped that if we keep practicing consent, we will keep learning what it feels like when we're in consent, and when we're not, or when we, or someone else, is overriding our consent. *The Wheel of Consent* website includes lots of videos and activities for getting used to what it feels like to tune into our wants and needs, limits and boundaries, and to communicate about these with another person.

MJ wrote a zine with a checklist for consensual relationships. You can find a link to the full zine in our further resources. For now, take a look down the list. Consider one of your close relationships. Which points on this list would you say are usually present between you? Which do one or both of you find harder? You can zoom in to explore particular encounters or interactions between you, or zoom out to consider the relationship as a whole.

1. *Consent as the aim:* Do we made consent the explicit aim of our relationship rather than one or both of us getting the things that we want, or giving the other person what they want?

2. *Informed consent:* When we arrange things between us, is everyone fully informed about what's being asked for, offered and so on, why, and where everyone is coming from? Is this true for the relationship as a whole?

3. *Ongoing consent:* Is consent ongoing before, during and after our encounters, and throughout the relationship? Do we keep checking in with each other verbally and/or non-verbally to see how we are with things?

222

4. *Relational consent:* Is this a relationship where everyone can bring their needs and limits, wants and boundaries to the table? Do we both feel free and safe enough to do so, knowing that we'll be heard and respected?

5. *Consent and wanting:* Are we able to clearly express and be heard about what we want and don't want, as well as what we consent to and don't consent to? Are we clear about who it is for?

6. *Multiple options beyond a default script:* Are we aware of the default script for "success" in this relationship—and in encounters between us—and have we shifted this to be open and flexible to multiple options, and an agreement to default to whatever is the lesser one that one of us wants?

7. *Power awareness:* Are we aware of the cultural and personal power imbalances between us and their potential impact on capacity to feel free enough and safe enough to consent?

8. *Accountability:* Can we notice when we've been non-consensual, name that with the other person (if they're up for it), hear the impact and offer to make reparations?

You might want to chat about this together with the people you're in close relationship with, and make some plans for how you might cultivate the capacity of each of you to be in consent within that relationship.

In addition to relationships being consensual, another useful concept here is intentional relationships. This means that rather than falling into the cultural ideal or community assumption of what a friendship, working relationship, romantic partnership, sibling or parent–child relationship should be like (for example), we get intentional about how we want to do that relationship between us. Often the goal is to make it as mutually nourishing, consensual and caring as possible.

This involves communicating with ourselves about how we want our relationships to be, and communicating with others in our lives about what they want and where our overlaps are. It relates to consensual relationships because it's about not falling into taken-for-granted assumptions about what our relationship should be like, because that is one of our worldviews, or because it's always been that way in the past, for example.

Make your own relationship user guide

A useful idea for getting intentional about relationships is the relationship user guide. This is similar to the idea we gave you in Chapter 16 about creating a body user guide, or the WRAP plans we touched on in Chapter 5. We can make user guides about all kinds of aspects of our self-care. This one is about how we like to do the relationships in our lives. The idea is to share it with people we're in close relationships with to prompt ongoing communication.

Here are some ideas for sections you might like to include in your user guide, but what you include is up to you. You can make it as a computer document, a series of note cards, a zine, whatever you like. If you want more prompts, MJ has written a zine which you can fill in with our great friend Justin Hancock. This is listed in the resources at the end of the workbook.

- What kinds of things are you looking for from relationships (mind map or word cloud)?

- What are your relationship values (see end of Chapter 21)?

- What are the essential elements of a relationship for you? Does this differ for different kinds of relationships?

- What styles or structures of relationship work best for you?

- Who are the key relationships in your life currently at different levels of closeness?

- How separate or together do you like relationships to be? What things would you like to share in some/all relationships?

- How do you like to share time and space in relationships?

- What is your relationship history?

- What are your relationship patterns that you're aware of? How do you like to navigate those?

- What are your expectations and hopes for how relationships will develop over time?

- What are your relationship boundaries (see Chapter 21)?

- What are your green, amber and red flags in relationships: the things that you love, feel uncomfortable with and are hard limits for you in terms of dynamics and behavior?

- What are your love languages: how do you like to give and receive love?

- How do you like to communicate? How do you like to deal with conflict?

The idea of intentional relationships can be helpful in reminding us that just because we feel a certain way towards someone—or have a certain history with them—this doesn't mean we have to have a certain kind of relationship. Rather, it's great if we can cultivate the container for this relationship that makes us most able to be kind and consensual with each other, to support each other in our projects, and to care for each other—and ourselves—in sustainable ways. It's OK—in fact, expected—that these things will change over time.

Of course, as we're sure you are aware, close relationships can be hard, extremely hard at times.

- We are all dealing with the human tension that we're driven by the desire to be free and by the desire to belong. This tension plays out all the time in our close relationships as we struggle with how separate and together to be with each person, how to balance our need for safety and security with our need for independence and relating with other people too.

- Dominant culture gives us a model of relationships—and everything— which is about getting what we want, and not what we don't want. This means that it's very hard to engage in relationships with open hands, rather than in a grasping manner. Most of us find ourselves tipping into either trying to get what we want from our people or trying to turn ourselves into what they want by losing ourselves. Authors such as Simone de Beauvoir, bell hooks and Erich Fromm talk about how we might move to a more mutual way of relating, where we value ourselves and others equally, but this is not easy in a culture that encourages us to do otherwise.

- Dominant culture also puts particular kinds of relationships—love relationships, parent–child relationships and, to some extent, friendships— under huge amounts of pressure. Our partner, parent, child or BFF is often expected to be everything to us, to complete us, to meet all of our needs.

Under such pressure, it's easy to experience a lot of loss as relationships don't measure up, to become disappointed and resentful, to stay in damaging relationships or to expect way too much of ourselves.

· We all bring our past relationship dynamics into each close relationship: the survival strategies, trauma responses and relational patterns which we've developed over time. When we're unaware of these—and even when we are aware—they can be hard indeed to navigate as we trigger each other or hit each other's buttons.

What particularly pressures have you felt in your close relationships? What kinds of tensions or conflicts often come up for you?

. . . .

. . . .

. . . .

. . . .

. . . .

. . . .

. . . .

. . . .

. . . .

We have both written a lot about managing conflict elsewhere, and there is not space to cover it properly here. Check out Alex's (2021) *Do Conflict Better!* and MJ's (2018) *Rewriting the Rules* in the further resources.

∽

CHAPTER 24

Building Self- and Other-Caring Communities and Cultures

Given that we understand ourselves as embedded within a network of close relationships, communities and institutions, and wider culture, all of these things are required to support us in self- and other-care. Sadly, for many of us growing up in criticism culture, they did the opposite, and this may still be true today.

Before we start this chapter, you might like to return to our familiar diagram. In what ways have the different layers enabled or discouraged self-care in your life? You might like to consider them in the past and now.

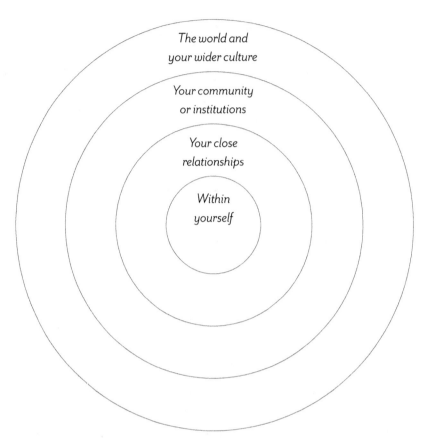

In the past

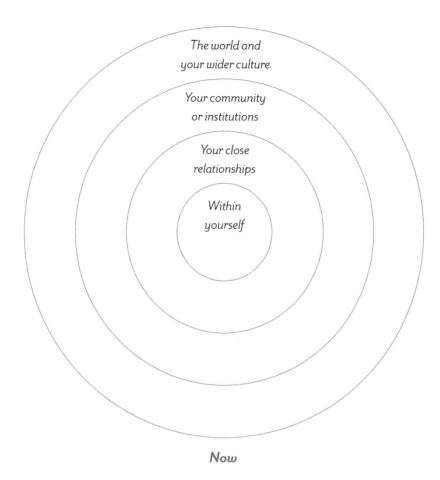

The world and your wider culture

Your community or institutions

Your close relationships

Within yourself

Now

We need systems and structures of support for self- and other-care, and we can't do it alone if our close relationships, our communities and institutions and our wider micro and macro cultures don't support it. It's also very hard to do if we're just embedded within small systems such as couples or nuclear families, without much support beyond these units. We like this phrase we heard from scholar Mimi Schippers (2019): "It's about developing networks of mutual care and responsibility."

Building sustainable, mutual, caring relationships, communities and cultures feels particularly important at times of ecological and economic crisis, and when so many of us have mental and physical health struggles related to trauma and the toxic cultures around us, and may need support when we're in crisis, sick, burnt out or unable to engage with work or look after ourselves in some ways.

In the last chapter, we dealt mostly with the level of close relationships and how these can support self- and other-care. In the rest of this chapter, we'll encourage you to consider how you might cultivate communities and cultures of support around you and your close relationships, and think about how you might develop these to be sustainable over time.

Communities and institutions

What systems and structures of support for self- and other-care are already happening for you at this level? Which ones might you like to cultivate more? You might like to note down or draw the ones that are already present on the left-hand side, and the ones you'd like to develop on the right of this diagram.

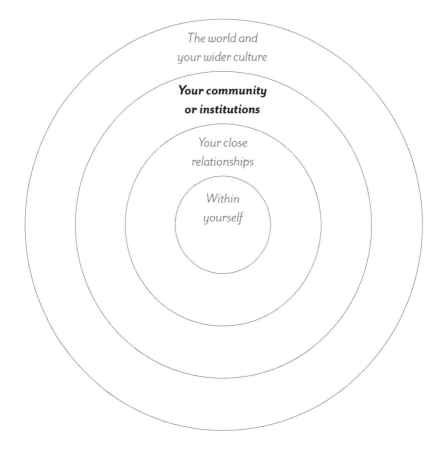

Here are some ideas that you might want to consider around cultivating community and institutions to support self- and other-care. Of course, these will not be relevant—or possible—for everyone, and you may well think of others that work better for you.

- If you don't have existing communities or friendship networks, look into developing these. You might consider how best to find people who share your values and are keen to develop mutually supportive communities. For example, consider existing spiritual and political groups, local meet-up and discussion groups, online groups around shared identities, experiences or intersections, finding friends through existing friends with shared values, or using friend/dating apps to make connections with like-minded people.

- If you do have existing friends and relationships, start having conversations about how you might like to build networks of care and sustainable communities together.

- Consider the institutions that you currently engage with—work, groups and so on. In what ways are these in line with your values? In what ways not so much? Which support you in self- and/or other-care and which make this difficult? What kind of work life would you like in terms of self- and other-care? What might be possible or ideal to shift into, and how might you go about this, perhaps gradually, over the coming years?

- Think about your living situation in a similar way. In what ways does this support you in your values and your self- and/or other-care? In what ways not so much? What kinds of living situation might you like in order to support you in your values and your self- and other-care? You might find it interesting to consider some of the possibilities that others are exploring, such as networks of care, queer kinship, communal and co-op living, various forms of co-parenting and sharing responsibility for children and animals.

- Explore forms of regular communities and groups coming together which you might bring in. This could include heart circles, reading groups, sharing circles, discussion groups, consensus decision making, mediation processes, accountability processes, group rituals and celebrations.

- Get involved in group activism around issues you care about, training and education, or listening to or supporting others.

- Facilitate events for like-minded people, if nothing already exists, or invite other people to come and do so.

Like close relationships, we're sure you are already aware that community and networks can be very hard indeed. If you're not, then trying some of the above will certainly teach you that lesson in pretty short order!

As in close relationships, in groups we often bring in those ways of relating that we've learned from wider culture: trying to get we want and not what we don't want, pressuring it to be perfect or meet all our needs, attempting to control or lead the group. We also bring our specific past dynamics and survival strategies into the group, and groups tend to develop their own dynamics which can get stuck, meaning that the group becomes dysfunctional, individuals get scapegoated or become too powerful and controlling, and so on.

We've listed some resources at the end of the workbook for navigating groups, networks and community. It's particularly vital here to recognize that people have been cultivating caring communities for a long time in various settings. Often, we've lost touch with traditional ways of doing this in dominant culture. In addition to developing new processes, rituals and structures, it's important to look to existing wisdom on this, as and when appropriate.

The world and your wider culture

Looking out to the world and wider culture, we've spent a lot of this workbook talking about the ways in which dominant culture discourages self- and other-care. Indeed, structures and systems such as the education system, criminal justice system, employment system, healthcare system can make self- and other-care hard, even impossible, at times, especially for those who are most marginalized by structural racism, misogyny, ableism, ageism and so on.

However, we can think about culture on a more micro level. What are the cultures available to us—for example, through engaging with certain forms of media rather than others, or through engaging with communities that are trying to create different micro cultures? How might we access cultures more in line with our values and worldviews—either existing cultures or co-creating new ones?

What systems and structures of support for self- and/or other-care are already happening for you at this level? Which ones might you like to cultivate more? You might like to note or draw the ones that are already present on the left-hand side, and the ones you'd like to develop on the right of this diagram.

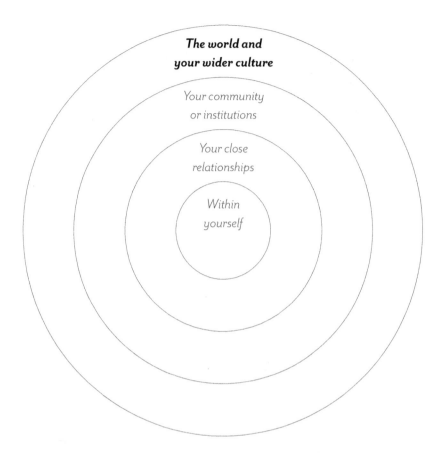

Here are some ideas that you might want to consider around micro and more macro cultures to support self- and other-care. Of course, these will not be relevant—or possible—for everyone, and you may well think of others that work better for you.

- Curate your social media accounts to engage with others who particularly support self- and/or other-care, developing mutual relationships and sustainable communities. You might think about who you follow in terms of being supported by others and about offering support, particularly across forms of injustice which both do and don't impact you directly.

- Consider the ways in which you engage with popular culture. What kinds of news do you want to take in? What kinds of representations do you want to see? What kinds of diverse voices and experiences do you want to engage with?

- Make art, zines, podcasts, videos, music, poetry or fiction about the kinds of things covered in this workbook and about your experiences, which you can share with others.

- Contribute articles or create blog posts or websites about these themes for other people to read.

- Write letters to newspapers, TV companies or advertising standards authorities about their representations.

- Write and speak to politicians and law-makers about relevant policies and laws which you think would be worth changing.

- Make yourself visible as someone who is doing things differently and is content with that. Ensure beforehand that you have the energy required to do this, as well as access to support if you do face criticism for it, and that others in your life are willing for you to do it, if it means identifying them too.

- Go on marches and protests against injustice or towards different ways of living and relating that resonate for you.

You might also consider ways in which you could practically help those around you to find the time and resources for their own self-care. This is part of creating micro self- and/or other-caring cultures. For example:

- Look after their people or animals or spaces to give them time.

- Give up your seat so they get to sit.

- Offer support or listening.

- Give practical help based on skills that you have.

- Amplify their voice/s online.

- Take on some of their battles (if they'd like that).

- Learn about being a helpful ally.

- Create resources.

- Set up groups.

M.Y.O. Slow Down Page

How might you slow down in community?

Who might support you to slow down

and how?

Reflections and Resources

Reflections

In this final section of the book, we're giving you a series of worksheets for reflecting on what you've learned over the course of the book and planning your self-care from now on. We hope these will help you to gather together your ideas and think about where you go from here.

We've included worksheets for addressing blocks and obstacles to self-care, figuring out your values and boundaries, planning your self-care for everyday life and specific circumstances, planning your life—and addressing the systems and structures around you—from the perspective of self-care, and regular check-ins to revisit and revise your thinking and practices. The section ends with some ideas about letting go and trusting the process.

As with the rest of this book, you can use these worksheets alone, or come together with others to engage with them. They might be helpful to work through and discuss, perhaps one per week in a sharing group. They could also be useful to share with your support network and encourage them to share with you.

It's often useful to start from what gets in the way of doing what we want to do. How many times have you had a plan or intention and found yourself unable to follow through? We invite you to see all that as information. Given that we've repeatedly talked about viewing emotion as information, and spoken about this as a self-acceptance process, it's just as important to accept the obstacles in our way, and trust that they have something to say to us.

Sometimes that information can be as simple as: "It's not your fault, there are forces and systems much bigger than you at play here. It's OK to just focus on the little bit that you can control." So, without further delay, let's take a moment to review which obstacles you may have found as you engaged with this workbook. For this worksheet, you may want to refer back to reflections and questions from Chapters 6, 7 and 19, or start fresh—it's up to you.

Take some time to list, draw, make a mind map or a collage—or whatever makes sense to you—of all the blocks and obstacles that get in the way of you being able to care for yourself and others. We encourage you to divide these into two categories: internal and systemic. For example, internal blocks might be feeling that taking time off is a privilege that too many other people don't have; systemic blocks might be not having paid sick leave or vacation time at work.

Systemic obstacles	Internal obstacles

Now that you've identified and summarized your obstacles, after engaging with this workbook, take a moment to notice what is and is not under your control. Please note that often our systemic and internal obstacles are connected. We hope that, ultimately, this helps you notice how challenging it can be to take care of yourself and others in a world that does not support interdependence and care. We also hope this helps you be kinder to yourself if your self-care doesn't look as you think it "should" look.

Now that we've looked at obstacles again, let's take a moment to go back to values. Remember the exercises in Chapters 7 and 21? You can also start from scratch!

If you're starting from scratch, you might want to first take the following steps:

- Jot down all the values you can think of, that you believe in.

- Sort those values into groups, such as most important, fairly important and low importance.

- Rank the values from your most important and fairly important groups. It's OK to have several values at the same ranking. For example, honesty and integrity might both be your number 1 values.

If you've already identified your defining, essential values in Chapter 7, and your relational values in Chapter 21, you may want to skip the steps above and go straight to the following activity for this worksheet.

Take some time to write your *Values Manifesto* on the next page. Imagine that someone is asking you to share what you believe in, which values guide you in life and what values you base relationships on. This manifesto would be your answer. It's a document in which to declare to yourself, and the world, what values are important to you. You can write it down, draw it, record it, make a collage or zine, or whatever else might work for you

My Values Manifesto

Now that you've got obstacles and values down, let's take a moment to revisit boundaries. You may want to refer back to Chapter 21 for this one, especially if you need a reminder of what boundaries are, and of the different types of boundaries.

First of all, write five to ten boundaries that are important for you to keep with yourself, for your own wellbeing. For example, one of them could be "I will brush my teeth every night" or "I will not work when I am sick."

Boundaries for my wellbeing

. . . .

. . . .

. . . .

. . . .

. . . .

. . . .

. . . .

. . . .

. . . .

Now write five to ten boundaries that are important for you in relationships. You may want to do this exercise a few times for different kinds of relationships, similar to what we suggested in Chapter 21. For example, one of them could be

"I will address conflict directly" or "I will ask for what I need while knowing and accepting I might hear 'no' in response."

Boundaries for my relational wellbeing

. . . .

. . . .

. . . .

. . . .

. . . .

. . . .

. . . .

If you want, you can also take time reviewing these boundaries and deciding which ones are most important to you. For example, are there relational boundaries that are "deal-breakers" in relationships of any kind?

. . . .

. . . .

. . . .

. . . .

. . . .

Finally, if you want to, you can also explore those boundaries somatically—that is, in your body. Here's one way in which you might want to try to do this. This is an exercise from Pat Ogden's somatic therapeutic approach, called Sensorimotor Psychotherapy (2015). Of course, you can use any of the other somatic practices mentioned in this workbook to explore your boundaries as well.

- Write down one of your boundaries on a piece of paper. Relational boundaries might lend themselves best to this exercise, but you can choose any of them.

- Create a circle on the floor around your boundary. You can use anything to create that circle such as yarn, chains, chalk, thread, jumping ropes, elastic bands and so on. Think about what kind of material would *feel* best for this boundary. This is highly subjective. Think also about how much space you want around that boundary, how large you want the circle to be.

- Once you have set the circle, go and sit with your boundary, inside the circle, and name your boundary out loud. Notice what comes up when you do this. You might want to use the FEAR or focusing practices described in Chapter 11.

- If you want, you can ask a trusted person to do this exercise with you and let them come right up to your boundary and stop just outside it. If this feels too close, you may want to make your boundary larger and then repeat the process.

- Do these for as many of your boundaries as you want to.

Here is a space to write about the kinds of self-care practices you'd like to put in place on a regular basis (see Chapter 8). Remember to be realistic about the time and energy you have, balance different forms of self-care (e.g. solo and with others, still and moving, kind and reflective), and go with practices that are a "yes" to you so you'll manage to do them.

My Self-Care Plan

Daily

. . . .

. . . .

. . . .

. . . .

Weekly

. . . .

. . . .

. . . .

. . . .

Monthly

. . . .

. . . .

....

....

Seasonally

....

....

....

....

Yearly

....

....

....

....

On-the-spot when I feel strong feelings/Reactivity

....

....

....

....

Here is a space to reflect on what the most self-caring practices are for you when particularly challenging times hit, so that you can revisit this if and when those things happen (see Chapter 8). Think about how you'd like to treat yourself—and be treated by others—at such times. What things help and hinder? What might you stop doing at such times, what additional things might you do?

When I get sick

Stop doing	Start doing

When a crisis hits

Stop doing	Start doing

When a big change happens
(e.g. moving, changing job, relationship change)

Stop doing	Start doing

When somebody in my life needs a lot of support

Stop doing	Start doing

When I'm grieving a loss or ending
(e.g. of a relationship, a dream, a project, during bereavement)

Stop doing	Start doing

In addition to the kinds of plans you covered in the last two worksheets, you might want to think about bigger changes that you could make in your life to improve the structures and systems of support around you for self- and other-care (see Chapters 23 and 24). Such changes may well need to be gradual over a period of years, rather than sudden.

My support network

What does your current support network look like?

. . . .

. . . .

. . . .

. . . .

In what ways does this help or hinder you in self- and other-care?

. . . .

. . . .

. . . .

. . . .

What would you like your support network to look like (e.g. in five to ten years' time)?

. . . .

. . . .

. . . .

. . . .

What steps might you take to shift towards this?

. . . .

. . . .

. . . .

. . . .

My living situation

What does your current living situation look like?

. . . .

. . . .

. . . .

. . . .

In what ways does this help or hinder you in self- and other-care?

. . . .

. . . .

. . . .

. . . .

**What would you like your living situation to look like
(e.g. in five to ten years' time)?**

. . . .

. . . .

. . . .

. . . .

What steps might you take to shift towards this?

. . . .

. . . .

. . . .

. . . .

My work/life projects

What do your current work/life projects look like?

. . . .

. . . .

. . . .

. . . .

In what ways does this help or hinder you in self- and other-care?

. . . .

. . . .

. . . .

. . . .

What would you like your work/life projects to look like (e.g. in five to ten years' time)?

. . . .

. . . .

. . . .

. . . .

What steps might you take to shift towards this?

. . . .

. . . .

. . . .

. . . .

This worksheet gives you a set of questions that you might like to ask yourself—and each other—regularly, in order to check how your self-care is going. It could be useful to put a date in the diary alone—or with friends—to do such a check-in once a season, for example. Or you might make it part of a reflection on the past, present and future on a key date like your birthday, or a new year reflection.

Past self-care

What were your main self-care practices over the last period (e.g. daily, weekly, etc.)?

. . . .

. . . .

. . . .

. . . .

Which ones did you find easy? Which ones did you find hard?

. . . .

. . . .

. . . .

. . . .

How easy or hard was it to find time and energy for self-care over the last period?

. . . .

. . . .

. . . .

. . . .

Easy ————————————————————————————————— Hard

What were the main blocks and obstacles (internal and external) to self-care for you?

. . . .

. . . .

. . . .

. . . .

Did you go through any particularly challenging things which meant you had to adjust your self-care (e.g. sickness, crisis, transition)? In what ways did this play out?

. . . .

. . . .

. . . .

. . . .

What systems and structures of support did you access around your self-care and how was that?

. . . .

. . . .

. . . .

. . . .

How gentle to harsh were you when you struggled with self-care over the last period?

Gentle ———————————————————————————— Harsh

Looking back to your past self, going into this period, what would you like to say to them?

. . . .

. . . .

. . . .

Future self-care

What are your self-care priorities going into the next period?

. . . .

. . . .

. . . .

. . . .

**What would you like your self-care practices to be
(e.g. daily, weekly, etc.)?**

. . . .

. . . .

. . . .

. . . .

**In what ways do you want this to change from the last period?
In what ways should it stay the same?**

. . . .

. . . .

. . . .

. . . .

**What do you imagine the main blocks and obstacles (internal and
external) will be for you? How might you approach these?**

. . . .

. . . .

. . . .

. . . .

Are there any predictable challenging things coming up which mean
you'll need to adjust your self-care (e.g. sickness, crisis, transition)?
What plans might you put in place for this?

. . . .

. . . .

. . . .

. . . .

What systems and structures can you access to support you in self-care
and how?

. . . .

. . . .

. . . .

. . . .

How might you be kind with yourself around self-care in the
coming period?

. . . .

. . . .

. . . .

. . . .

Looking forward to your future self, at the end of this period, what would you like to say to them? What do you imagine them wanting to say to you now?

. . . .

. . . .

. . . .

. . . .

Well, this is a lot of reflection that you may just have gone through. We've offered a lot of ideas, practices, exercises and worksheets. There are also further resources at the end of this chapter. This can all feel a bit much. I don't know about you, but we felt a little inadequate by the end of writing this self-care workbook. We definitely don't do all the things covered in this workbook all the time ourselves! And you know what? That's absolutely OK. Because, in the end, these are just ideas and tools. If they help us, that's great. However, if we feel overwhelmed by them, or we end up feeling bad about ourselves, then it means they're not helpful, at least not right now.

So, take as deep a breath as you can, that's great… Now let's do it again.

Breathe in all of these ideas and exercises and work you might have done

And

Breathe out and let it all go…

Yes, you read that right. Let it go. Let what is helpful be there and be of use. Let go of the rest, maybe even all of it right now.

It's OK if you're just surviving right now, for example, and can't do any of it, or only some of it. It's OK if this feels overwhelming right now. It's OK if you need to rest, digest, or whatever else you need to do with these materials.

Let it all go….

And trust. Trust can be a hard one for us, so we encourage you to look at trust as a practice. You don't have to be perfect at it, or even close to good at it; you just need to be willing.

Trust yourself and trust those around you, if they're worthy of trust. It's also OK to make mistakes and discover you've trusted the wrong people and start again. You can always come back to that cradle of kindness we mentioned in Chapter 4.

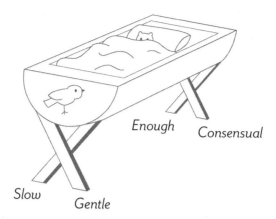

Enough   *Consensual*

Slow   *Gentle*

Remember those four elements that supported the cradle of kindness? Here they are in case you need reminding:

· Go *slow.*

· Be *gentle.*

· You're *enough.* We're *enough.*

· *Consent* with ourselves and with others.

And if this feels like a lot, let it go too and always come back to the breath.

Resources

Further resources

Here we've listed further resources that you can access around various aspects of self-care relating to the different themes we've covered in this workbook, including the ones we've touched on in various chapters.

Self-care in general

Adams, K. (2009). *Journal to the Self*. New York, NY: Grand Central Publishing.

Barker, M-J. (2017). *Hell Yeah Self Care*. www.rewriting-the-rules.com/zines.

Barker, M.J. (2015). *Social Mindfulness*. www.rewriting-the-rules.com/zines.

Barker, M.J. (2019). *Regret Ritual*. www.rewriting-the-rules.com/self/regret.

Barker, M.J. and Iantaffi, A. (2017). *How to Understand Your Gender*. London: Jessica Kingsley Publishers.

Barker, M.J. and Iantaffi, A. (2019). *Life Isn't Binary*. London: Jessica Kingsley Publishers.

Batchelor, M. and Batchelor, S. (2001). *Meditation for Life*. Somerville, MA: Wisdom Publications.

Bernhard, T. (2018). *How to Be Sick: A Buddhist-Inspired Guide for the Chronically Ill and Their Caregivers*. London: Simon and Schuster.

Engaged Mindfulness Institute (2019). https://engagedmindfulness.org.

Kline, N. (1999). *Time to Think: Listening to Ignite the Human Mind*. London: Hachette.

Lorde, A. (2012). *Sister Outsider: Essays and Speeches*. Berkeley, CA: Crossing Press.

Lorde, A. (2017). *A Burst of Light: and Other Essays*. NY: Dover Publications Inc.

Lorenz, T.N. (2017). *Aggressive Self-Care. A Digital Coloring Book*. https://blog.spoonieliving.com/post/162054105485/the-aggressive-self-care-coloring-book.

Mason, M. (1990). "The Myth of Independence." In R. Rieser and M. Mason (eds), *Disability Equality in the Classroom: A Human Rights Issue*. London: Inner London Education Authority.

Ortiz, N. (2018). *Sustaining Spirit: Self-Care For Social Justice*. San Francisco, CA: Reclamation Press.

Staying with feelings

Ahmed, S. (2010). *The Promise of Happiness*. Durham, NC: Duke University Press. https://feministkilljoys.com.

Barker, M-J. (2016). *Staying With Feelings*. www.rewriting-the-rules.com/zines.

Chödrön, P. (2010). *The Wisdom of No Escape*. Boulder, CO: Shambhala Publications. https://pemacho-dronfoundation.org.

Cornell, A.W. (2000). *The Power of Focusing*. Thinking Allowed Productions. https://focusing.org, www.focusing.org.uk.

Fredman, G. (2004). *Transforming Emotion: Conversations in Counselling and Psychotherapy*. London: Whurr. www.taosinstitute.net/about-us/people/institute-associates/europe/uk/glenda-fredman.

Gendlin, E.T. (1964). "A Theory of Personality Change." In P. Worchel and D. Byrne (eds.), *Personality Change*. NY: John Wiley & Sons.

Gendlin, E.T. (1982). *Focusing*. NY: Bantam.

Marlatt, G.A. and Gordon, J.R. (1985). *Relapse Prevention: A Self-Control Strategy for the Maintenance of Behavior Change*. NY: Guilford Press.

Neff, K. and Germer, C. (2018). *The Mindful Self-Compassion Workbook*. New York, NY: Guilford Publications.

van Deurzen, E. (2008). *Psychotherapy and the Quest for Happiness*. London: Sage Publications. www.emmyvandeurzen.com.

Somatic self-care and trauma

Adler, J. (2002). *Offering from the Conscious Body: The Discipline of Authentic Movement*. New York, NY: Simon and Schuster.

Allen, J.G. (1999). *Coping with Trauma: A Guide to Self-Understanding*. Washington, DC: American Psychiatric Publications.

Haines, S. (2015). *Trauma is Really Strange*. London and Philadelphia, PA: Singing Dragon.

Kain, K.L. and Terrell, S.J. (2018). *Nurturing Resilience: Helping Clients Move Forward from Developmental Trauma—An Integrative Somatic Approach*. Berkeley, CA: North Atlantic Books.

Levine, P.A. (2008). *Healing Trauma: A Pioneering Program for Restoring the Wisdom of the Body*. Boulder, CO: Sounds True.

Maté, G. (2010). *In the Realm of Hungry Ghosts*. Berkeley, CA: North Atlantic Books.

Maté, G. (2011). *When the Body Says No: Exploring the Stress-Disease Connection*. New York, NY: Wiley.

Ogden, P. and Fisher, J. (2015). *Sensorimotor Psychotherapy: Interventions for Trauma and Attachment*. New York, NY: W.W. Norton & Company.

Raffo, S.: Blog posts on healing justice, trauma and collective liberation: www.susanraffo.com/blog.

Schwartz, A. (2017). *The Complex PTSD Workbook: A Mind-Body Approach to Regaining Emotional Control and Becoming Whole*. Berkeley Press, CA: Althea Press.

Taylor, S.R. (2018). *The Body is Not an Apology: The Power of Radical Self-Love*. Oakland, CA: Berrett-Koehler Publishers.

Van Dernoot Lipsky, L. (2009). *Trauma Stewardship: An Everyday Guide to Caring For Self While Caring for Others*. Oakland, CA: Berrett-Koehler Publishers.

van der Kolk, Bessel, A. (2015). *The Body Keeps the Score: Brain, Mind, and Body in the Healing of Trauma*. New York, NY: Penguin Books.

Walker, P. (2013). *Complex PTSD: From Surviving to Thriving: A Guide and Map for Recovering from Childhood Trauma*. Createspace Independent Publishing Platforms.

Plural selves and selves-in-process

Barker, M.J. (2018). *Plural Selves*. www.rewriting-the-rules.com/zines.

Barker, M.J (2019). *Plural Selves FAQ*. www.rewriting-the-rules.com/self/plural-selves-faq.

Bazzano, M. (2016). "The Fourth Treasure: Psychotherapy's Contribution to the Dharma." In R.E. Purser, D. Forbes and A. Burke (eds), *Handbook of Mindfulness*. Cham: Springer.

Burr, V. and Butt, T. (1992). *Invitation to Personal Construct Psychology*. London: Whurr Publishers.

Butt, T. (2003). *Understanding People*. Basingstoke, Hampshire: Macmillan International Higher Education.

Gergen, K. (2001). "Self Narration in Social Life." In M. Wetherell, S. Taylor and S. Yates (eds), *Discourse Theory and Practice: A Reader*. London: Sage.

Peyton, S. (2017). *Your Resonant Self: Guided Meditations and Exercises to Engage Your Brain's Capacity for Healing*. New York, NY: W.W. Norton & Company.

Plummer, K. (2002). *Telling Sexual Stories: Power, Change and Social Worlds*. London: Routledge.

Plural Positivity (2019). *Plural Positivity World Conference*. March 30th, 2019, www.systemspeak.org/ppwc.

Redwoods: website on plurality. https://redwoodscircle.com.

Rowan, J. (2013). *Subpersonalities: The People Inside Us*. London: Routledge.

Rowan, J. and Cooper, M. (eds) (1998). *The Plural Self: Multiplicity in Everyday Life*. London: Sage Publications.

Stone, H. (2011). *Embracing Your Inner Critic: Turning Self-Criticism into a Creative Asset*. New York, NY: Harper Collins.

Stone, H. and Stone, S. (2011). *Embracing Ourselves: The Voice Dialogue Manual*. Novato, CA: New World Library.

Schwartz, R.C. and Sweezy, M. (2019). *Internal Family Systems Therapy*. New York, NY: Guilford Press.

White, M. and Epston, D. (1990). *Narrative Means to Therapeutic Ends*. New York, NY: W.W. Norton & Company.

White, M. (2007). *Maps of Narrative Practice*. New York, NY: W.W. Norton & Company.

Close relationships, consent and conflict

Barker, MJ. (2018). *Rewriting the Rules: An Anti-Self-Help Guide to Love, Sex and Relationships*. London: Routledge.

Barker, M.J. (2018). *The Consent Checklist*. www.rewriting-the-rules.com/zines.

Barker, M.J. and Hancock, J. (2016). *Make Your Own Relationship User Guide*. www.megjohnandjustin.com.

Barker, M.J. and Hancock, J. (2017). *Make Your Own Sex Manual*. www.megjohnandjustin.com.

Barker, M.J. and Hancock, J. (2018). *Sex: A Practical Guide*. London: Icon Books.

Graham, S. (2019). *Love Uncommon*. https://oveuncommon.com.

hooks, b. (2018). *All About Love: New Visions*. New York, NY: William Morrow.

Iantaffi, A. and Effinger-Weintraub, L. (2020). *Do Conflict Better*. Transforming Perspectives LLC.

Iantaffi, A. (2020). *Why Did You Bring Me A Dead Bird?* A zine about trauma and relationships. https://www.alexiantaffi.com/resources

Martin, B. (2019). *The Wheel of Consent*. https://bettymartin.org and https://schoolofconsent.org.

Mingus, M. (2011). *Access Intimacy: The Missing Link*. https://leavingevidence.wordpress.com/2011/05/05/access-intimacy-the-missing-link.

Systems and structures of support

Berila, B. (2016). *Integrating Mindfulness into Anti-Oppression Pedagogy*. New York, NY: Routledge.

brown, a. m. (2017). *Emergent Strategy: Shaping Change, Changing Worlds*. Chico, CA: AK Press.

brown, a. m. (2019). *Pleasure Activism: The Politics of Feeling Good*. Chico, CA: AK Press.

Building Accountable Communities: https://survivedandpunished.org/2018/09/27/building-accountable-communities.

Byrd, R.P., Cole, J.B. and Guy-Sheftall, B. (2009). *I Am Your Sister: Collected and Unpublished Writings of Audre Lorde*. New York, NY: Oxford University Press.

Chen, C.I., Dulani, J. and Piepzna-Samarasinha, L.L. (eds). (2011). *The Revolution Starts at Home: Confronting Intimate Violence Within Activist Communities*. Brooklyn, NY: South End Press.

Clare, E. (2015). *Exile and Pride: Disability, Queerness, and Liberation* (reissue edition). Durham, NC: Duke University Press.

Clare, E. (2017). *Brilliant Imperfection: Grappling with Cure*. Durham, NC: Duke University Press.

Owens, L.R. and Syedullah, J. (2016). *Radical Dharma: Talking Race, Love, and Liberation*. Berkeley, CA: North Atlantic Books.

Piepzna-Samarasinha, L.L. (2018). *Care Work: Dreaming Disability Justice*. Vancover: Arsenal Pulp Press.

Schippers, M. (2019). *Polyamory, Monogamy, and American Dreams: The Stories We Tell about Poly Lives and the Cultural Production of Inequality*. London: Routledge.

Transform harm: https://transformharm.org.

van Dernoot Lipsky, L. (2018). *The Age of Overwhelm: Strategies for the Long Haul*. Oakland, CA: Berrett-Koehler Publishers.

Our further resources

You can find out about our other books, podcasts, and other resources on our websites.

Alex Iantaffi
Personal website: www.alexiantaffi.com
Podcast: genderstories.buzzsprout.com

Meg-John Barker
www.rewriting-the-rules.com
https://megjohnandjustin.com

By the same authors

How to Understand Your Gender
A Practical Guide for
Exploring Who You Are

Alex Iantaffi
Meg-John Barker
Foreword by S. Bear Bergman

£14.99 / $19.95 | PB | 288 PP | ISBN: 978 1 78592 746 1 |
eISBN: 978 1 78450 517 2 |

Have you ever questioned your own gender identity? Do you know somebody who is transgender or who identifies as non-binary? Do you ever feel confused when people talk about gender diversity?

This down-to-earth guide is for anybody who wants to know more about gender, from its biology, history and sociology, to how it plays a role in our relationships and interactions with family, friends, partners and strangers. It looks at practical ways people can express their own gender, and will help you to understand people whose gender might be different from your own. With activities and points for reflection throughout, this book will help people of all genders engage with gender diversity and explore the ideas in the book in relation to their own lived experiences.

Life Isn't Binary
On Being Both, Beyond, and In-Between

Meg-John Barker
Alex Iantaffi
Foreword by CN Lester

£14.99 / $19.95 | PB | 240PP | ISBN: 978 1 78592 479 8
eISBN: 978 1 78450 864 7

Much of society's thinking operates in a highly rigid and binary manner; something is good or bad, right or wrong, a success or a failure, and so on. Challenging this limited way of thinking, this ground-breaking book looks at how non-binary methods of thought can be applied to all aspects of life, and offer new and greater ways of understanding ourselves and how we relate to others.

Using bisexual and non-binary gender experiences as a starting point, this book addresses the key issues with binary thinking regarding our relationships, bodies, emotions, wellbeing and our sense of identity and sets out a range of practices which may help us to think in more non-binary, both/and, or uncertain ways.

A truly original and insightful piece, this guide encourages reflection on how we view and understand the world we live in and how we all bend, blur or break society's binary codes.

Gender Trauma
Healing Cultural, Social, and
Historical Gendered Trauma

Alex Iantaffi
Foreword by Meg-John Barker

£19.99 / $27.95 | PB | 224PP | ISBN: 978 1 78775 106 4
eISBN: 978 1 78775 107 1

Exploring how the essentialism of the gender binary impacts on clients of all genders, this ground-breaking book examines how historical, social and culturally gendered trauma emerges in clinical settings. Weaving together systemic ideas, autoethnography, narrative therapy and somatic experiencing, the book charts the history of the gender binary and its roots in colonialism, as well as the way this culture is perpetuated intergenerationally, and the impact this trauma has on all bodies, gender identities and experiences.

Featuring clinical vignettes, exercises and reflexive practices, this is an accessible and intersectional guide for professionals to develop their understanding of gender-derived trauma for supporting clients. Highlighting the importance of applying a trauma-informed approach in practice, this book provides insights as to how we can work towards collective healing, for future generations and for ourselves.